An Inside Job

ROBERT C. WITT

WinePress Publishing
MUKILTEO, WA 98275

Library of Congress Catalog Card Number: 97-60087
ISBN 1-57921-004-X

FOREWORD

This story is true. The events and dates recorded are accurate throughout. Names of many people and several places have been changed or deleted to protect the innocent and obscure the identity of those whose behavior did not reflect credit on their character. After repenting of my own bad behavior and finding God's forgiveness, I have no desire to cause pain or embarrassment to others.

I earnestly hope that everyone who reads about my exploits as a thief, burglar, safe cracker, and escape artist will realize that I deeply regret my criminal behavior. Anyone who is enamored with my adventures and tempted to copy some of my techniques should think again. That would be a terrible mistake.

I am writing, first of all, to challenge public officials to view their words and actions from the criminal's perspective. I hope they will recognize that even criminals and convicts respect fair judges, truthful lawyers, humane police, and compassionate guards and prison officials. When I was treated with cruelty and dishonesty by those in positions of power over me, my rebellion increased. When I was treated fairly by the authorities, I could no longer justify my blaming society for the bad behavior I myself had chosen. I hope and pray that those in power today will heed the words of Chaucer: "*If gold rusts, what will iron do?*"

Secondly, I want my story to encourage youthful readers to profit from my mistakes. I have been an expert at making bad decisions, usually based on indecision, desire for acceptance, and lack of defined goals. I hope that adolescents with these same tendencies can master their lives better, and sooner, than I did. My journey of torment began with youthful rebellion and violation of the Fifth Commandment: *"Honor your father and your mother ..."* (Exodus 20:12).

I am also telling my story to provide hope for incarcerated inmates who long to leave prison, yet fear what awaits them on the outside. If my story helps just one convict break the pattern of crime and recidivism, it will have been worth all the effort.

Finally, I am writing to express gratitude to Almighty God for His abounding love and unfailing guidance *"...through the valley of the shadow of death"* (Psalm 23:4). I rejoice to say with King David: *"My cup runneth over"* (Psalm 23:5).

Robert C. Witt

CONTENTS

GUILT AND PLEADING
An Awesome Choice

The long night had been sleepless, as Betsy and I tossed and turned, paced the floor, and prayed. The early morning was no less stressful, as we prepared to call the lawyer and give him our dreaded decision. I recalled his statement in his office the previous day: "Let's face reality, R. C. The Port City authorities are looking for a guilty plea, and they'll give you a sentence of only twelve months to get it. That's their bottom line and it won't get better."

I replied that I would have to discuss it with Betsy and sleep on it. He responded, "You've got until eight o'clock in the morning to give them your answer or the deal's off; they made that clear."

When I first told Betsy, she screamed, "No! I don't think it's a good deal! You don't realize what we went through for three and a half years without you, and they don't care what it has taken to get our lives back together during the past ten months you've been home! And now they're saying we'll have to start all over again!"

In my head I knew the lawyer's assessment was accurate, but emotionally I agreed with Betsy. For ten months they had kept us in a state of suspended animation. I felt that if they really believed I was guilty they would not have bartered down from fifteen years, to ten, to five, and finally to just twelve months. It was quite apparent they knew their case was very weak and that they could be embarrassed by a "not guilty" verdict.

On the other hand, a new trial might find me guilty again and sentence me to another thirty years. I remembered with bitterness how they had wrongfully convicted and imprisoned Betsy with no real evidence whatsoever, and my blood ran cold at the realization of their power. As I had once said, "Make 'em mad enough and they'll do anything they want to you."

I'll never forget Betsy's final statement as we agonized over our decision: "R.C., no matter what decision you make, I do not believe God is going to allow you to go back to prison. He would never have let you come home just to make you go back. He doesn't work that way. He'll work another miracle just like He did before."

A sentence of twelve months was surely better than fifteen or twenty years, but I still had deep-seated apprehensions and anxieties. If the judge decided to reverse the deal negotiated by the prosecutors, I would be completely at his mercy. I could only imagine the impact another long prison term would have on my son, Tucker. Fortunately, he had been too young to comprehend the significance of prison when he visited me at Powhatan, referring to it as, "The place where Daddy used to work."

It would be different for Tucker now, however, as he had become old enough to understand the stigma and feel the pain. His three-year-old exuberance on the first day of my release still echoed in my mind: "Daddy, do I really get to keep you now?"

Just a few minutes before the 8:00 A.M. deadline I turned to my wife and shared what had suddenly become clear to me: "Betsy, have you ever been convicted about a certain thing because it was the right thing to do and you knew you had to do it? I don't know how it is going to work out, I know what it means to you and Tucker, and I know the dread I feel about it, but I'm convinced in my heart that accepting this deal is the right thing to do. I was involved in the crime; I was a professional thief. Bypassing alarm systems and cracking safes was as natural to me as a part-time job. The underworld was the only place I felt at home, living by the outlaw's code of ethics.

"All that is over now. I am a new man, a new creation, and I'm trying to think like the new person, not the old. Some right decisions are hard to make in life, and I want you and Tucker to feel confident that you can count on me to make the right decisions, no matter what it may cost.

"You remember how, when we started this seemingly impossible journey with the Lord, we learned the `Trust me' principle? Well, all of a sudden I now feel confidence in my heart as I hear, `Trust me; trust me'!"

I finally called my lawyer on his private line. Knowing I was the caller, he began, "You're a last-minute kind of guy." When I told him my decision he seemed relieved that we would not have to go through an ugly trial as before.

"Be in my office by ten o'clock," he said. "We'll be in front of the judge in closed court by eleven, and it'll all be over." He made it sound like having a tooth pulled.

Sitting there in the court room, surrounded by a few close friends and family members who came to give us moral and spiritual support, we silently waited for the judge to arrive. As I mused on the high stakes of that day's trial, my mind drifted back over my three decades on and off the merry-go-round of crime. How did it all begin? What went wrong? Such reflection led me all the way back to memories of my teenage years, beginning with a Saturday night visit to my church...

CHAPTER 1

PRE-SCHOOL OF CRIME
JUVENILE DELINQUINCY, 1962-68

I used to marvel at being in our church when no one else was there. Typical of most Catholic Churches of an earlier era, it had beautiful stained glass windows, big wooden doors, a ceiling that seemed to me to be three stories high, and a long center aisle that made its way to the red-carpeted steps ascending to the altar.

The altar seemed spooky, yet holy. Made of dark marble, it looked like some sort of sacrificial table, with candles and brass fixtures on top, and the ever-mysterious tabernacle, no more than a foot or so high and wide. This held the very Body of Christ, the Eucharist, at least during Mass. Or so I had been taught.

Most overwhelming of all was the huge cross behind the altar where our Lord hung grotesquely from huge nails the size of railroad spikes. The cruel crown of thorns, from which drops of blood dripped down His face, was pressed into his scalp. His head hung down as if He anticipated the spear that would pierce His side.

In my sheltered young life I couldn't imagine anyone ever doing anything like that to another human being. And to my astonishment, as I had learned in my catechism, He was not only innocent of any crime, He was the best person who ever lived. God become flesh, full of love, even loving the very executioners who nailed the spikes through His hands and feet.

This incredible revelation was to become my first insight into the reality of human nature. Depraved people interpret kindness as weakness and nail others to a cross, without mercy or compassion. They seem driven by an obsession to make others suffer. Although I have pondered this phenomenon all my life, it still defies my comprehension. How could anyone find such perverse pleasure in inflicting pain on One so innocent and helpless?

On this particular occasion I didn't just wander into the church during quiet hours; I had specifically come for Saturday night confession. Each penitent would stand in line with five or six others, waiting to go into the dark confessional, kneel, and recount hidden sins. When my turn came, I began with the customary, "Bless me, Father, for I have sinned."

At fourteen years of age, I suddenly discovered my confession had become a dialogue with the priest behind the screen. To my horror, he wanted to know what kinds of impure thoughts I had that would consign me to hell, and why I said I hated my father. I did not like either topic, but at least I could talk about the latter.

At the conclusion of this very uncomfortable conversation, the priest recommended that I come see him at the rectory after school to discuss my troubled relationship with my father. Afraid to say no, I accepted the appointment. Several days later I found myself sitting face-to-face with the priest, in a room off the rectory.

My initial discomfort was soon replaced by shock and fear, as I felt the holy father put his hand on my leg. At first I wasn't sure what was happening, until he started moving his hand. I thought I would die right there in the chair. I could not believe what was happening, and I wanted to get out of there immediately. To my great relief, a knock at the door caused him to release his awful grip on my thigh and retire from the room to answer a call. In his absence I quickly made my escape, telling the rectory maid it was past time for me to go home. This incident shattered my spiritual and moral well-being.

My mind was reeling all the way home. I was sick with shock and wanted the whole awful scene out of my mind. In addition to this trauma, I was grieving over the death of my best friend, my dog. He had been following me while I was delivering newspapers and had darted in front of a speeding car that abruptly ended his life. The car sped off as if nothing had happened, leaving me with feelings of intense bitterness and isolation. I began to express that bitterness and rebellion in antisocial behavior that produced great trouble.

A year or so later, after extended family consultation, it was decided that everyone would be much better off if I left home and moved in with my oldest sister, Brooke, whom I called, Miss Brooke. Her husband was the meanest man I had then met, even meaner than my dad, although in a different way. My dad seemed to me to be meaner psychologically, while Bob, my sister's husband, was mean both mentally and physically.

I often wondered how my sweet, gentle, wonderful sister could have ever loved and married this dictatorial bully. He was a smooth-talking, domineering man who climbed the ladder of financial success the Dale Carnegie way, suavely manipulating others. Everyone in his house was required to begin and end each day by reading a chapter of a Carnegie book.

Bob also loved to fight. This was repulsive and demeaning to me, weighing about 115 pounds compared to his 230. Beginning playfully, he often became brutal. Years later, when forced to fight for my life during my first term in prison, I was grateful for those earlier lessons in self-defense. But as a lonely teenager, my hatred of Bob made me determined to be free of his oppression. I hated fighting and did not want a dictator controlling my life. Under the guise of freedom, I went off with a street friend to steal a car and head for parts unknown.

One might expect my experiences in Juvenile Detention Center to shock me into righteous living, but it was in that very place I first stepped onto the perilous merry-go-round of crime that kept me going in circles for over two decades. Like a billiard ball ricocheting on a pool table, I reacted aimlessly in response to external forces. To get away from juvenile probation I joined the Marine Corps. Like everything else in my former life, it just happened that way, with little thought and no goals.

Home on a three-day pass from the Marine Corps, drinking with old friends, I was arrested on the beach with three cases of long-neck Budweiser beer stolen from a local restaurant. After sixty days in jail, the judge sentenced me to one year in jail, reduced it to a misdemeanor, and suspended the remainder of the sentence so that I could return to military duty.

Because my sixty days in jail was unauthorized absence from the Marine Corps, I was incarcerated in a nearby brig. Old Marines can testify as to what brigs were like in 1966, far more terrible than almost any civilian jail anywhere in the country.

It was there that I attempted my first escape from confinement. Working the garbage detail, I observed the way garbage was carried from the compound. At the gate, two MPs would climb up the side of the trash truck with a long poker and poke around in the refuse, then allow the truck to pass through the gate. I noticed that the pokers weren't long enough to reach the bottom. And because the garbage on the bottom was so putrid, I concluded that the guards would never expect anyone to crawl down into it.

Following my analysis of the situation, a sailor, also assigned to the brig garbage detail, joined me in a bid for freedom. At the appropriate moment we jumped on the truck and quickly burrowed our way to the bottom of the rancid garbage. The truck was soon off the compound, but it was moving too fast for us to jump onto the highway. By the time we could jump off we were inside the dump and seen by the driver. He sounded the alarm as we sprinted toward freedom.

The farther we ran, the more we became bogged down in a marshy swamp. Within a matter of minutes helicopters loaded with Marines soon had us back in custody. We were handcuffed, thrown in a van, and beaten with billy clubs and fists all the way back to the brig. I remember wondering why they were so angry. Why were they so vicious and cruel? Then, for a split second, I had a flashback of God-become-flesh nailed to that cross by His own creatures, hanging above the altar in Holy Trinity Catholic Church.

Our captors put us in dark little cells, naked, with nothing in the cell except a hole in the floor. I soon figured out what the hole was for. Even though I could not see it, the stench it sent up was so vile and oppressive I could hardly breathe.

After eating nothing but bread and water for two weeks, I was shipped to a brig at Camp LeJeune, North Carolina. Conditions there were so barbaric that I gladly accepted an administrative discharge which stated, "Convicted of a felony by civilian authorities." That was not really true; I was convicted of a misdemeanor, not a felony. The lieutenant explained that acceptance meant immediate freedom, whereas contesting the charge would require me to languish in that God-forsaken brig for another two months. Considering the alternatives, I accepted the erroneous indictment, left the Marine Corps, and drifted back to civilian life.

Coming home was extremely depressing. Everyone in my family seemed to look upon me with utter disdain. I now realize how deeply I had disgraced them. My parents reared seven children and worked diligently for all of us. My father continually struggled just to stay one step ahead of the bill collectors.

Now that I am off the merry-go-round of crime I understand my father much better than I did then. He undoubtedly felt constant fatigue, oppression, and depression, laboring from sunup to sundown to feed, clothe, and educate so many children, one of whom claimed to hate him. In retrospect, I don't believe I really hated him as much as I resented him for shutting me out and failing to give me the acceptance I craved. Years later I grew to love him.

My father's father had abandoned him and the rest of his family when my dad was very young. My grandfather was also a mean alcoholic. So, despite my father's failings, he was still a great improvement over his father.

As the middle child of seven, I believe I somehow got in the way of my parents' relationship. It seemed that when I could occasionally get close to my dad everything somehow went wrong between them. Consequently, I learned to keep my distance.

One thing that has always impressed me about my father is the appreciation and respect conferred on him by all his associates outside the family. Throughout my entire life people in all walks of life who knew my father have given me preferential treatment simply because I was his son. I've never heard anyone outside my family say a bad word about him.

Shortly after my discharge from the Marine Corps, I began seeking a place to stay and searching for my old friends. I expected them to welcome me with open arms, and I was not disappointed. The first one to greet me was my closest friend at that time, Harold. He and I became known as the "vending machine bandits." We fleeced all types of coin machines and usually had four or five hundred dollars in change at any given time.

I somehow persuaded my mother to co-sign for me to buy a 1962 Chevy Super Sport, the joy of my life at that time. It was fast, looked sharp, and was the means of freedom and revelry.

At eighteen years of age, I had been in and out of the Marine Corps, in and out of several jails and brigs, and was living in my own apartment. I owned a fine car and had more money than any of my friends. It was during that time that I met and married my first wife, Sandra, despite the fact that I was totally unprepared for such commitment and responsibility.

I thought I was happy and felt pleased with myself. However, my freedom abruptly ended when I was arrested for possession of stolen goods obtained through the burglary of a drug store. Going to jail this time gave me a real scare and prompted some genuine soul-searching. When no one seemed interested in getting me out,

I became very depressed and even thought about suicide. Sandy somehow raised the money needed for my bond and I was released.

Sandy and I drifted from place to place, staying with one friend here and another there, waiting in limbo for my trial. During that time I stayed away from all wayward friends and acquaintances. I truly wanted to quit hustling and reorder my life with purpose and productivity. Additional motivation came when Sandy announced her pregnancy. I could feel the responsibility mounting; I was concerned, fearful, and filled with self-doubt.

My family obtained a lawyer who was a friend of a cousin, who was also a lawyer. The attorney told me there was no way I could beat the charge, but if I would plead guilty he could get me ninety days in jail, and I'd have to do only sixty. This was two weeks after Sandy and I went to visit my family at a beach cottage.

On our first day at the beach cottage I was informed that Sandy and I were not welcome. My father explained that they had rented the cottage for my sister, Lucy, and her husband and their friends. Intellectually, I realized the cottage was indeed too crowded; emotionally, I was deeply hurt at being rejected and expelled. My response to rejection has always been an attitude of indifference and nonchalance, either real or pretended.

When the court day finally came, I kissed Sandy goodbye and told her, "Hang in there and I'll see you in a couple of months." After going through court procedures the judge sentenced me to ninety days and placed me in the custody of the sheriff. I was anxious to get it all over with. Then, three days later, I was called to appear in circuit court. I told the deputy there must be some mistake; I had already been to court. But it was no mistake. I went before another judge who had, over a year earlier, given me a suspended sentence. With no lawyer, no testimony, or even the right to plead my case, this judge sentenced me to twelve months, running consecutively with the three months given two days earlier.

The judge explained that it wasn't really a trial but a revocation hearing of the one-year suspended sentence he had previously imposed on the condition that I would not commit another crime. When I had pled guilty to the charge of petty larceny in exchange for a sentence of ninety days in jail, my prior probation was revoked and the original sentence of one year was activated.

I called Sandra and gave her the bad news. A week later I was boarded on the "long chain" and delivered to a living nightmare. At the age of eighteen I was viewed by the old convicts as fresh meat. As I came through the gate of Powhatan Prison, then known as the State Farm, I could hear their cat calls coming from the many steel-framed windows. I thought I was going to be sick.

I was taken to the basement, stripped, doused with a bucket of vinegar and given a shower, all in an open area with sex perverts looking on with sick smiles on their faces. I heard one convict say, "What kind of judge would send a young kid like that to a place like this?" I knew then I was in trouble. Fear gripped my heart like a vise and my ears rang. I kept telling myself I must hang tough, I must keep my guard up.

I was placed in a dormitory just before a ninety-man work detail returned for head count. They were a motley collection of humanity, these old and middle-aged men in brown uniforms, with scars and tattoos on their bodies and hate in their eyes. Several glanced at me with twisted smiles on their faces as they went by.

After head count was completed, a hustler I had done time with in the North Fork Jail came up and welcomed me. I was so happy to see a familiar face that I had to catch myself to keep from showing too much appreciation. Steve gave me the rundown on how to act, who to watch, and he ominously advised, "Get yourself a knife. In fact," he said, "I'll get one for you." I prayed to wake up from this nightmare, but I wasn't sleeping. It was all too real.

Going to the mess hall, I recognized another inmate I did time with in North Fork, a young guy like me. I soon noticed something strange in the way he looked. Then I realized he was walking with "his man." He had been "turned out" in homosexual hell.

At night I hardly slept, and when I did it was with one eye open. I was placed on a "shot gun gang," going out the gates to work in the fields for fifteen cents a day. The gang captain pushed us to the limit so miserably that I was ready to run, even if it meant getting shot. Every day I looked for a chance. Every day I anticipated they would call me to the office and tell me my time had been suspended and I could go home. That day never came.

The only time I was called to the office was to be informed that my wife had given birth to a baby girl on January 10, 1968. She was named Robin Michelle. I didn't even want to think of my precious daughter while I was in that God-awful place. I didn't want to use the same brain to comprehend such total opposites as new life and dead existence.

With "good time," a convict can serve ten months and get credit for fifteen, but even ten months seemed an eternity. It was early in that ten-month stint, while shoveling cow manure with my gang in the barn, that a black inmate suddenly attacked me. We fought and rolled in manure for several minutes until the gun guard finally stopped it. It was evident that I got the best of him.

Because I was young and skinny, I originally assumed he had spontaneously spotted me as an easy mark, but I later discovered his attack was instigated. My opponent was so humiliated that a young skinny white boy had "kicked his butt" that he tried to stab me with a pitch fork when I wasn't looking. Another black man yelled a warning just in time, and the pitchfork stuck in the wood of the stall where I had been working. The black man who had alerted me later warned, "Never turn your back on a Nigger after you just whipped him." I wasn't sure if he was trying to scare me or give me good advice, but I remembered what he said.

Immediately after we returned for the evening, another convict approached me, an older man who had been down for over sixteen years. He offered to settle my score for me, acting like he was my friend. I replied that I didn't think the guy could stand another lost fight, and the old-timer stared at me real strange. Later I learned that this same older inmate, who offered to settle my score, had paid the black dude to beat me up. He had planned to follow my beating by acting as my avenger and we would then become "friends." Obviously he had not expected me to come out on top. Initially I wondered how he knew so quickly there had been a fight. Then I realized it was all the result of his evil conniving.

There were all kinds of games like that. Young guys were tricked and traded. Fortunately, my early fight won me enough respect to handle the later conflicts. I saw several men cut and stabbed to death. Another hanged himself. Two escapees were shot dead and thrown on the back of a truck like sacks of potatoes.

During those long months I began to think that I would never live to see my release date. And if I did, I would be so full of contempt and hate that I would be somewhat insane. While I was there I made new criminal connections and learned new tricks that later promoted my pursuit of crime. After that stint I hated society a hundred times more than when it began. That is what happens to convicts in prison. As I rode the bus back to North Fork on March 6, 1968, I pondered the events of that terrible sojourn and realized that I would never again be the same.

HIGHER EDUCATION IN CRIME

POWHATAN AGAIN

Coming home, March 23, 1968, was a joyous experience—like resurrection from the dead. For the first time I focused attention on my daughter. She was two months old and very beautiful, and the sadness of missing her birth was replaced by the happiness I felt holding her in my arms. Despite the tender feeling for my infant daughter and wife, however, my commitment to them did not sufficiently motivate me to become a law-abiding citizen. I still did not support them by the sweat of my brow. After graduation from my first school of crime I had a rebellious heart and felt driven to get even for the misery I had endured in prison.

It is hard to describe how I felt. It was not an emptiness because I was filled with pain, sorrow, resentment, anger, and humiliation. The humiliation was worse than when I came home from the Marines, yet, like then, I was back at my parents' home. They had been kind enough to keep Sandy and the baby from the time they came home from the hospital, converting the upstairs into a small apartment. I occupied the same room in which I grew up, but now with Sandy and my daughter. I knew I had to get away from there.

Throughout all my family relations, I felt a profound sense of failure. I didn't want to see anyone who knew me, except my street friends. I felt accepted and valued only with them.

I had several menial, low-paying jobs with little opportunity for advancement, but without transportation I had to hitchhike to and from work, losing up to four hours daily. My self-reproach and anger rendered me impatient and unable to recognize my own capabilities. Looking back now, I believe I could have worked my way up in several of those jobs if I had stuck it out. Years later I repeatedly surprised myself with my determination and ability to get things done. But as long as I believed I was an ignorant, worthless failure, my overt actions expressed such negative self-image and fulfilled my negative expectations.

Sandy, the baby, and I moved into a basement apartment on West Ocean View, where the James River and Elizabeth River empty into the Chesapeake Bay. I spent many a night on that beach alone, lost in thought. It was a refuge where I searched for the meaning of life's perplexities. I've always loved the water—rivers, beaches, and oceans—and the water always provided the habitat for tranquil reflection and hope.

Our financial plight was so bad that my mother-in-law often bought us groceries. Fortunately, I was able to save enough money to buy an old used car. Unfortunately, the car became the source of trouble, as well as transportation to work. Strange things began to happen surrounding that old clunker.

I was not surprised to see the police following me one day. When a convict is released from prison he is required by law to report to the local police exactly where he lives and works. They keep the ex-con under surveillance, and often, as in my case, they let him know it by overt, needless harassment. Before I went to prison they regularly had me under surveillance because of my trifling reputation. After I became clean, I had no reason to believe they would pull me over without cause. But I was wrong; they did. And when I reached for my wallet and discovered I had left it at home, I felt an ominous anxiety. They arrested me for operating a motor vehicle without a license and impounded my car. Sandy brought my license to court the next morning, and the judge fined me $25 and court costs for not having it with me.

By this time the landlord was tired of police intrusion and asked me to leave. I took Sandy and the baby and stayed with the wife of an incarcerated friend. She was glad to have company while her husband, one of my old hustling partners, was doing time at a road camp.

A few days later I stopped off to cash my paycheck at one of the old watering holes where I had been drinking since I was fifteen years old. Al, the owner, cashed my check and I settled down on a stool with my beer. Al told me that two detectives had been there asking for me. Because I had not recently done anything wrong, I was naively unconcerned about their inquiries. I told Al to earn himself some brownie points by calling them. I sat there drinking beer while waiting for the police to come.

When they came, it was not the customary harassment and questioning; to my amazement, they arrested and jailed me for a burglary that happened more than two years earlier. Because the burglary occurred while I was in the Marine Corps brig, the case was ultimately dismissed. Nevertheless, it cost me my job and quite a bit of money I did not have for a bondsman and a lawyer.

Every time I went to retrieve my impounded automobile something else seemed to go wrong. When I finally raised the money and appeared at the holding garage, I was informed that the car was being held in an investigation. When I asked, "For what?" no one knew; it was just written on the card, "Hold until Detective E. authorizes release." I then hired a lawyer to force the old car to be released. This unwarranted harassment cost over two hundred dollars, two weeks' time, and great frustration.

In the meantime, on a Friday night, I had some friends over for beer and snacks and to watch a television movie. We were never loud or wild; we just talked, watched TV, and drank some beer. Around midnight all my friends but one had gone. He fell asleep in the chair, and I dozed on the couch after Sandy had gone upstairs to bed. The TV was still on, but the station had signed off for the night. The front door was open but the screen door was shut and hooked. It was a warm summer night.

I was awakened by someone beating on the door. I got up, walked to the door, and saw two detectives standing there, demanding that I let them in. When they refused to tell me what they wanted, I replied that they should get a search warrant. They responded by violently yanking the door open, throwing me to the floor, and putting a gun to my head. I watched in disbelief as more than a dozen others poured into my living room.

They tore the apartment to pieces, waking the baby and scaring Sandy and my friend's wife. After searching every inch of the house and coming up empty, they carted me off to jail where I was booked for disorderly conduct. I sarcastically asked: "Was I snoring too loud?"

I was extremely angry over this incident and decided to fight it in court. By this time I was seeing my lawyer once a week. He advised me more than once to go to another town to start over. He said the police would never rest until they had me back in prison. I was too naive and foolhardy to believe him; I never thought they would actually be so vindictive. Only twenty years old, I had committed no heinous crime worthy of notoriety or persecution. I expected they would leave me alone because they had more important things to do.

As strange as it may sound, I began to feel a weird satisfaction in the reputation the police were creating for me by their unwarranted harassment. Hustlers I hardly even knew began to seek me out and treat me with deference. Either willfully or unwittingly, the police were helping advance my criminal career.

As I made new friends in the criminal world, I found such associations challenging. I experienced an unseen bond with those peripheral offenders who enjoyed the adventure of non-violent crime while maintaining a semblance of personal morality. It was as if we recognized and understood each other as fellow travelers from the world of misfits.

As time passed, I discovered that the worst kind of friend to have is a crook. No matter how tough and loyal I thought they were, they always seemed to break under police interrogation. They not only "spilled their guts," they even lied about partners, bargaining for their own freedom by concocting imaginary stories with no factual base. Despite all their macho pretense, it is usually true that "there is no honor among thieves." With few exceptions, the ones who talked, looked, and acted the toughest usually turned out to be the least dependable—and the most treacherous.

Two of the most despicable hustlers I ever encountered were Skippy T. and his partner, Butch. They had developed a check-cashing scam requiring a sucker like me. They didn't really respect me, as I first thought, but were simply using me. Just when I finally recognized the extent of their treachery, Skippy T. was arrested and told the police I was their ring leader. Thus, when I made another trip to the compound to retrieve my car on May 18, 1968, I was immediately arrested for several counts of forgery and for passing worthless checks. Thanks to Skippy and my own stupidity, my life continued on a steady downward slide in my twentieth year of existence.

Sandy persuaded my father to get me out on bond after announcing that she was again pregnant. Bond was set at seven thousand dollars. Although this was a small amount compared with the half-million-dollar bond I would face in New Mexico twenty years later, it taxed his resources both financially and emotionally. Out on bond after two arrests, I did finally get my car, but the money paid for legal fees and bond left me very frustrated and deep in debt.

A week after my release, my friend Sonny, then on the run for six months, called me needing help. He had skipped bond on a burglary charge and had hooked up with some professional thieves out of New York. A bust had split them up and now Sonny was lonely, needing a friend; I was that friend in his time of need. Afraid of going back to jail, I decided to run with him. I told Sandy I'd send for her when we settled down.

Sonny and I zigzagged down the east coast, going inland through Tennessee and Georgia and eventually making our way to Miami. All along the way we cased places commensurate with our criminal skills and hit the easiest. Sonny had indeed learned some new tricks from his friends in New York and gladly shared his skills with me. We partied quite a bit, something Sonny never omitted for more than a few days. One bar we entered was so rowdy that even most of the bikers avoided it; that kind of place was just right for Sonny, so in we went.

After conversation and a dozen drinks with Joe, the bar owner, Sonny told him he had some gold pieces he was trying to unload. Joe's eyes lit up and he told us to go get them and bring them into his office so he could see them. "For the right price," he said, "I'll buy all you have."

I was very leery of Joe, not only because of the way he looked and talked, but because he knew we were strangers on his turf. Sonny derived a false sense of security from the .38 caliber snub nose pistol he carried in an ankle holster when he went to places like this. I often warned that some day it would cause him or someone else to get killed or hurt, but that night it probably saved our lives.

In the office we met Joe's partner, "Side Kick," who promptly pointed a big gun at us and took the little satchel of gold that we had previously stolen. He flashed the badge of a deputy sheriff, handcuffed us, and declared us under arrest. When they stuffed us in the trunk of their car, I knew he was a fraud.

My throat was so dry from fear I thought I'd choke, but even in the face of such a terrifying moment, Sonny blurted out, "Hey, Joe, I think this might be against my constitutional rights to be transported to jail like this," and then he laughed. It was probably because of his drunken condition, but I loved him at that moment. I loved him for easing the fear that gripped me. He relieved the tension of that terrifying night. I laughed with him, as Side Kick roughly pushed me in on top of my friend and slammed the trunk shut. At that moment I somehow knew we would live.

We knew we were following another car when Side Kick stopped along the road to discuss with Joe what route to take. Joe was in the lead car and was clearly in charge. As I felt Sonny reach for his ankle I remembered the gun. I remember thinking, "This is going to be interesting."

We turned off the main highway onto a bumpy dirt road that felt like a bike trail. Every time the driver hit the brakes the inside of the trunk would glow with a red light that enabled me to see Sonny's sweat-drenched face and the gun held in both cuffed hands. He held the barrel up to his lips to signal silence, and his eyes were as big as saucers.

The car stopped and then backed up at an angle. My heart was racing as I heard Side Kick fumbling with his keys. The instant the trunk lid flew open everything happened as quickly and perfectly as if Sonny had planned and rehearsed it for a week. He popped up on his knees like a jack-in-the-box, thrusting the pistol in Side Kick's face so quickly that the barrel hit him in the teeth. The auto tail light revealed a look of shocked disbelief. Side Kick jumped back with his hands out and fell backward down a ravine he and Joe had undoubtedly selected as our grave site.

When Joe arrived from his car, he could not see what was happening because the trunk lid blocked his view. When he came around the side of the car he received the same shock, and revealed the same expression Side Kick had. With the gun barrel pointing between his eyes, held by a very angry man in hand cuffs, big mean-talking Joe slowly fell to his knees, tears streaming down his cheeks, begging Sonny not to kill him. It was pathetic how quickly this macho man revealed such bankrupt character, unable to take what he had dished out to his victims. I started to tell Sonny not to kill him, but then realized he wasn't going to anyhow.

Our suspicions that Joe and Side Kick had planned to rub us out were confirmed when we discovered that they did not even bring keys for the cuffs. We couldn't find Side Kick, although we heard him thrashing through the woods like a wounded deer. We locked Joe in his own car trunk by himself. To make sure he would stay there for a long time we pulled as many wires as we could from under the hood and took a handful with us. After driving away in our car, we stopped and removed the cuffs with our burglary tools.

Because I was afraid that Joe might suffocate in the trunk, and because Sonny wanted to go back for our gold, we returned to the scene of our near-death experience just in time to see the trunk open and Joe streak down the road as if demons were chasing him. He had somehow opened the trunk as we rounded the last turn, and he probably concluded we had come back to kill him as he had planned to kill us. He reminded me of a jack rabbit, running off the road and hopping through the weeds to avoid our headlights.

We found our little satchel of gold on the front seat. As much trouble as it had caused us, I almost wished it had been gone. Taking the pistol Sonny had confiscated from Joe, I vented my cockiness and relieved my tension by shooting out all the windows of his car. Relating the events of that night to other friends—bums like us—in later times, Sonny and I would laugh till tears streamed down our faces. After more somber reflection, however, the memories of that night's stark terror led me to realize how close we had come to getting killed or killing someone else. Surely the hand of God protected us in a very special way.

A few weeks later, in Tampa, Florida, I met Sandy and the baby at the airport near the Holiday Inn where Sonny and I were staying. As time passed, it became increasingly uncomfortable for all four of us to travel around together. Sonny solved that problem when he called his girlfriend, Anna, and she talked him into turning himself in. I took him to the airport and saw him off on a plane to Virginia. It was truly paradoxical how, just a couple of months earlier, he had talked me into running, but then quit running with me to turn himself in.

After Sonny's family hired a good lawyer, he was sentenced to only one year locally and had the charges dropped in New York. As always, he came out smelling like a rose; eight months later he was back on the streets, before I had even gone to court. I found it increasingly difficult without a partner, so I sent Sandy home with the car and set out on my own, broke, with no transportation and no plans. It seemed like life was just one big crap shoot.

In the midst of aimless isolation, I went to see a friend named "Wop," who sent me to see "Frenchy," and he placed me in the home of a bootlegger friend called "Peepsight." Peepsight got his name from a prison fight in which another inmate hit him in the head with a brick, severing an eye muscle and causing one eye to angle out. To focus his good eye he had to close the other one.

One day while I was at Peepsight's house a strange car pulled into his driveway and I hid in the closet while his wife answered the door. To everyone's humor and amazement, it was "Red" Lane and Wally, friends of Peepsight, who had just escaped from jail in Williamstown, Virginia. Even though they were out-laws—proficient thieves and gifted safe crackers—both Red and Wally were kindhearted to poor friends and got into more trouble helping other people than in seeking their own gain.

Six months earlier they had targeted the safe of a South Carolina Coca Cola plant. While they were open-ing the safe, the owner unexpectedly came in and called the police. Practically the whole town assembled with shotguns, surrounded the plant, and captured them. A month later a judge sentenced them to thirty years. Soon thereafter they escaped from the South Carolina Penitentiary by smuggling themselves out in a laundry truck. They made their way back into our state but were recaptured and locked up in the Richmond jail.

Because the Richmond jail was very secure and the one in Williamstown was not, they signed written con-fessions for a Williamstown crime they knew someone else had committed. They were promptly remanded to the Williamstown jail, from which they quickly escaped and came to Peepsight's house where I was also hiding.

Frenchy, Red, Wally, and I then took off together. Wally moved into a trailer park in Danburg, Virginia; Red and his wife, Pat, rented a place in North Carolina, where I often stayed. Frenchy remained in Beach County when he wasn't with us. Each of us would find a particular score, case it, plan it, and then call in the oth-ers to pool our skills to knock it off together. They were always safe jobs. Usually I was the "inside man" because I could climb with dexterity and quickly cut a hole through the roof. Red and Wally usually cracked the safe, while Frenchy was the "hawk." As time went on, we purchased two-way radios, police monitors, and other equipment that made our work safer and more efficient. Frenchy persuaded us that pickings were much better in North Fork and Beach County. Thus, in spite of the danger of recognition where I was well known, Red and I moved to Beach County for what was scheduled to be just a short while. I moved into an apartment with Sandy and the baby, while Red and his wife had an apartment several blocks away.

One day I called a fence in North Fork who ran a gun shop and was into all types of illicit activities. An ex-convict who had served eight years, he later married a girl who died in childbirth. Her tragic death left him psychologically impaired, and he was never again the same. Because he had a federal charge pending, he made a deal with the Feds to help catch me if they would drop charges against him. He told me it was extremely important that I see this girl we called "Sissi" and that she would explain everything when she saw me. Frenchy and I went together to the pre-arranged rendezvous point where about sixteen FBI agents were waiting.

After handing me over to the Beach County police, the Feds and some city cops went to the address they found in my wallet and found Sandy and my daughter. Red happened to drive by as they were raiding the house, and, thinking I was in trouble, he wanted to help me. The police became suspicious of the red Thunderbird that kept circling the block and pulled him. When they found a police monitor and a gun in Red's car, he too was arrested.

After a fingerprint check on Red revealed his identity, the police and newspapers had a field day. One thing led to another, and the pot really began to boil. An informer who knew Frenchy learned from him about our scores and began writing statements. The police persuaded him to change his wording from "I heard" to "I did," and he claimed that Witt, Frenchy, and others were with him. After his "confessions" he got probation for several charges of possession of stolen goods as a reward for his cooperation. Red beat his rap altogether. Frenchy got forty years but had it overturned by the State Supreme Court after just three years. I was sentenced to twenty years and served over twelve.

Several months after we were caught, Wally was arrested somewhere near Atlanta, Georgia. While in prison he discovered he could draw and actually became an accomplished artist. I heard he was later pardoned in South Carolina and became a devout Christian. At last report, he was making a living from his art and was married to a fine Christian.

I was sent to a road camp where I escaped and was recaptured the same day. After I was thrown in "the hole," Sandy sent me a "Dear John" letter; she was through with me, and I could not blame her at all. There seemed to be little hope for me—no basis to believe that I would ever amount to anything. She had the responsibility of two young daughters, she was young and lonely, and she deserved better than what I had given her. Even though I knew she had to divorce me, it was still hard to take. In October of 1970, already hurt by separation from Sandy and my daughters, I now felt I had lost them forever; it seemed there was less and less reason for me to go on living.

The day I got out of the hole I was cuffed and chained in the back of a pickup truck filled with chickens and hauled all the way across the state of Virginia to a road camp far up in the mountains near Tazewell. On the way, we stopped for lunch at another road camp where I got more bad news through the prison grapevine. Red had died of a heart attack in the Richmond prison.

I learned that Red at least had the comfort of dying with a true friend; Wally had carried him to the prison hospital after Red collapsed while jogging around the ball park. It was a hard blow to Wally and to me. Red had been in good shape the last time we were all together; I couldn't understand it. Prison life had been as hard on Red as it was on me. The constant stress, the helplessness, the prison gloom, and the poor diet all took their toll with the passage of time.

When I arrived at the Tazewell Camp I was numb, emotionally as well as physically. The camp captain introduced himself and led me away to his hole so that I would know what it was like. It really wasn't much different from the one I had just left.

After a couple of days in the hole I was assigned to a shotgun gang cutting the right-of-way for highways and power lines across the mountains. The first day after work I was called to the captain's office to hear his standard lecture against attempting escape. He claimed that the statistical success rate was zero; no one had ever made it out of *his* prison camp since he took over!

As the word spread that I had rabbit blood, another convict sought me out and said he was looking for a way out. I had smuggled some hacksaw blades in the binding of a book, and this was just what my new friend, Eddie, was looking for. Eddie worked in the kitchen where he immediately began cutting a bar out of the window in the store room. That evening, after he completed the cut, he and another convict who worked in the kitchen helped sneak me up to the store room. We did this by acting like

I was in the pill line, and when the guard was distracted I shot past him up the steps to the kitchen where Eddie was waiting for me. We were short on time since it was seven o'clock and they counted at seven-thirty, so we were in a hurry to get as much lead as possible. The space where the one bar had been taken out was so small we had to take our clothes off to squeeze through. At the last moment a young convict named Mick decided to go with us, so we waited for him before running for the main mountain ridge. Since we knew the mountains ran north and south, we planned to ascend the ridge top and turn south toward a highway and thus avoid aimless wandering. All three of us were from flat-land cities and knew nothing about the mountains. We had much to learn over the next three days, and we learned quickly.

We could hear the posse chasing us most of the night, their dogs barking wildly. Cars and trucks roared up and down the mountain roads, but before the night was over rain was pouring down. The rain washed away our scent, robbing the dogs of their effectiveness. The thick woods provided excellent cover, allowing us to put distance between us and our would-be captors. Two days and nights of continual walking and running without food left us exhausted, and the absence of warm clothing enabled the November mountain cold to penetrate our shivering bones. The renewed experience of freedom, however, made it all worthwhile.

Four days after our break-out we were heading back to Richmond in a stolen car, taking Mick to his mother's house. It seemed that Mick was heartsick and ready to quit. Sure enough, a few days later we heard that he was caught in his mother's house. Eddie and I split a couple of months later, and I was captured after another six months, visiting Red's widow near Richmond. An ex-convict had seen me driving Pat's car and turned me in to the Feds in exchange for reduction of counterfeiting charges then pending against him.

Because of my increased notoriety as an escape artist, the Department of Corrections then sent me to my old alma mater, Powhatan, for safe keeping. There I was immediately placed in maximum security for what the captain of security promised would be a long, long time.

Powhatan had a separate compound attached, where the laundry was located. The laundry was a big building with two loading docks for tractor-trailer trucks entering and leaving each day. Many inmates had tried to escape by hiding in the laundry and leaving under a loaded truck, but none were known to have succeeded. Security would not allow the trucks to leave until head count was clear, which meant that an escapee would have to beat both head count and the roster. Such a complicated procedure seemed impossible, yet some intuitive force led me to believe that I *could* escape, and that the laundry was the way to do it.

The industrial area was just as secure as the main compound, with double fences twelve feet high, topped by two-hundred-volt electric wire. Guard towers were at every corner of the middle fence line, manned by guards with high-powered rifles that had crippled and killed numerous inmates attempting to escape. There was another fence and guard tower that separated the main compound from the laundry, with a huge gate operated from the guard tower. When no one was in the laundry, the back towers were not needed and were left unmanned. Therefore, the rational conclusion was that a successful escape required beating both head count and the guard on the door of the laundry.

Based on this assumption, I worked out a plan to get into the laundry during working hours and hide, with a dummy placed in my bed that would hopefully pass head count. After a satisfactory head count, guards from the outer towers of the laundry would be removed. In the still of night, I could then come out, cut a hole in the fences, and leave. With my plan thus formulated, all I had to do was put it into action.

Regulations required inmates to stand during head count, but guards had become lax, often allowing them to lie on or in their beds during the 5 p.m. count. After work, many inmates would go in their cells, padlock their door, and go to sleep for a while. This was routine for those working in the kitchen and those with odd working hours. In light of this, I made a dummy by stuffing socks, pants, and shirt and by forming a head from wet newspaper mesh. I got a friend who worked in the barber shop to bring me some hair, which I glued on the head. I placed the dummy in bed, covered it so that nothing but hair showed, and hid under the bed.

As I lay hidden under my bed, sweat oozed from every pore of my body, expressing the intensity of my anxiety. If they found my dummy, I would be a marked man, but I felt that I had to test my plan prior to the actual day of escape. I waited breathlessly as the count guard ambled by, saw my dummy, and moved on. It was a tremendous relief, yet I realized I needed a back-up plan in case the count guards spotted my dummy while I was hiding in the laundry on the day of my bid for freedom. If they spotted the dummy at head count I wanted them to think I was already gone and not still hiding inside the prison.

I noticed that during lunch, when all inmates left their work areas to go eat in the mess hall, some guards who brought brown bag lunches would exit through a side door and walk down the sidewalk to the front gate. The guard on duty in the main control tower would let the other guards out by pushing a button in the tower, unlocking the gate, and allowing them to eat their lunches on the outside. Because there were many guards, and they all wore the same uniforms, I had at one time considered trying to walk out in a guard's uniform. I eventually abandoned this idea as being too risky in broad daylight. But if I could sandbag the prison administration into thinking I intended to make such an attempt, it could serve as a diversionary decoy in support of my actual plan.

I had a friend who worked in the tailor shop make and smuggle to me a complete guard's uniform. I then put it on top of some pipes I had sabotaged. This was done so that the inmate plumber, a known snitch, would find the uniform and report it to the security officer. Just as I had planned, the plumber came, repaired the pipes, and left. Within fifteen minutes the shakedown squad came and found the stash.

Since only five of us worked in that area and I was the only escape risk, they dragged me off to the Captain of Security. I knew he couldn't prove the stash was mine, so I stood there and listened to him tell me how he was aware of my plans to walk out of "*HIS*" gates posing as a guard. He threatened me with years of segregation if he could get proof of my plans and told me that my stupid idea would never work. How could I fail to realize he kept a more secure prison than that...etc., etc., etc.? Of course I denied any such plans and he sent me back to work with a few final threats. My back-up plan was complete. If they should find my dummy, I hoped they would think I had succeeded in walking out the gate posing as a guard.

Next, I had to figure out how to get off work early and into the laundry with none of the guards recognizing me. I also had to prevent other inmates from realizing what I was doing. Since I had once worked in the laundry, I knew all the procedures. All workers had to go in a side door where a guard checked them in and put them on the count. The number checked out had to be the same as the number checked in. At the front of the laundry there was a loading dock where trucks left their trailers full of state hospital laundry to be unloaded. One trailer was always there, to be unloaded on Tuesdays between three and four o'clock.

I planned to walk through the gate, holding a pass in my hand, as all inmates do when beginning a new work assignment or coming from sick call. Knowing there was no other way to leave the laundry, the tower guard assumed that anyone entering the laundry gate must work there. Tuesday had to be the day because the trailer was then loaded with laundry. Monday night, I showed my cell mate exactly how to place the dummy in my bed after he would come in from work on Tuesday evening.

Tuesday afternoon I secured a pass from work to see my counselor. Instead of going to the counselor's office, however, I calmly walked across the yard, hoping no one would recognize me, and stopped at the gate. For a second my heart came up in my throat when the gate didn't open. Finally, I heard the "buzz" of the electric lock as the gate opened! I walked through and closed it back. It was too late to turn back now.

I walked toward the side entrance of the laundry with my heart pounding in my ears. Glancing back to make sure the guard wasn't looking, I jumped up on the loading dock and walked to the back of the truck.

Opening the truck door, I climbed up on the canvas baskets of laundry and pulled the door shut behind me.

I stayed still for a few minutes to see if I had been seen, thinking that it would be a miracle if I hadn't. There were all kinds of open windows in the laundry and another guard tower at the truck gate from which the guard could see the loading dock. When the silent passage of time convinced me I was not observed, I climbed into one of the baskets. They were approximately three feet square, with wood skids on the bottom, a wood hinge on top, and steel bands on three sides. The soiled laundry was putrid, and I was lying on something wet. I covered myself with sheets and towels, and burrowed down as deep as I could.

After what seemed an eternity, I heard the steel doors open. I could feel the movement of the trailer as inmates slid the tongues of their hydraulic dollies under the baskets and wheeled them into the building. When they got to my basket they had to lower it by hand because it was piled on top of other baskets. I could hear the inmates swear and complain how heavy it was. Then they dropped the basket to the floor of the truck when another inmate crashed into it with his dolly. My head hit one of the steel bands so hard it made my ears ring. I no longer felt the previous wetness because my whole body was wet with sweat.

To complicate matters, they put my basket on the bottom of the stack. I lay there with both legs and feet completely numb from the cramped position in such a confined space. Finally, after about an hour and a half, the work bell rang, and the building became completely quiet. Soon thereafter, I heard the sound I was so intently anticipating: the big steel door slammed shut, signifying that everyone was gone. By this time my cramped legs ached terribly. I massaged them and flexed the muscles, only to have the numbness replaced by excruciating pain. I knew I had to get out of that laundry basket immediately. After several minutes of struggle I was grateful to be out, standing upright.

I fixed the baskets back as they were and searched for a hiding place in case they found my dummy. From the front windows of the laundry I could see the back of my cell block, and through those windows I could see the catwalk in front of the cell. Soon I saw the first count guard walk by and count the dummy. A few minutes later another guard passed my cell, hesitated, turned, and walked back. I knew it meant trouble. Within minutes guards were surrounding my cell and I could clearly see them drag the dummy out.

Now I was really scared. Within an hour, over a hundred guards were scurrying throughout the compound. They were on the roof tops and in the yard, prying up all the manhole covers. A helicopter marked "State Police" landed on the baseball field and took off for aerial observation of the surrounding countryside. As I observed all their frantic activity, I knew it would be only a matter of time before they would come search the laundry. There were only two ways to enter the laundry, either through the gate from the main compound or through the truck gate, both of which I could see.

After looking everywhere for a hiding place, I spotted a big steel filter on a platform in one corner of a very high ceiling. I removed my shoes, tied them to my belt loops, and climbed up two lengths of half-inch conduit that carried the electrical wires to the filter, gingerly using only my fingers and toes to support my total weight. The filter was round, about the size of a two-hundred-gallon drum. I wedged myself behind it for six hours while guards with dogs tore the laundry inside-out. The only place they didn't look was the place I was hiding. Even if they had looked, a long extension ladder would have been required to get to my perch. Fortunately for me, none of them thought to look up.

All the next day I stayed there while other inmates worked beneath me. I thought the heat would kill me before the day was over. When I had to urinate I was forced to simply wet my pants, but being so dehydrated, the quantity was not great. When the work day finally ended, I managed to climb down with great difficulty. Because my arms and legs were so rubbery weak I almost fell.

Knowing that security would not remove the laundry tower guards till they thought I was gone, I was determined to wait them out. Each day was spent hiding on my elevated perch; the darkness of night enabled me to climb down, drink water, relieve myself, and walk around. After four days without any food, I was very glad to see that the guards were removed from the rear towers. I feared it might be a trick to flush me out, but as soon as darkness fell I went for it.

Gingerly nursing a pair of wire cutters previously stolen from the electrical shop, I climbed up to the ceiling where only the ceiling windows were big enough to allow passage of a human body. I climbed through the window onto a lower roof and dropped to the ground. Feeling very vulnerable and anxious, I belly-crawled to the first fence and cut a hole in the chain link fence just large enough to squeeze through. Then I crawled the eight or ten feet to the next fence and repeated the same procedure. I was out of prison! Free once again!

Years later, I learned that the head of security did conclude that I had walked out the gate posing as a guard after all. In fact, prison authorities totally revamped security procedures because of my escape. My back-up plan had worked! Relief flooded over me in a way that defies description, that night of November 24, 1971. Even though I was twenty–three years old, much wiser and more hardened to prison life than during my first stretch, serving time was still a living hell. How wonderful it was to smell the fresh breeze gently blowing across the James River! Knowing that the railroad tracks parallel to the river led to Richmond, I walked and ran the twenty-five miles into the city, despite the weakened condition of my body after four foodless days.

I went to the house of an old girlfriend who provided me with food, sleep, clothes, and money. From there I went to Maryland, where I rented an apartment, found work, and obtained new identification credentials.

This process always begins with a fictitious birth certificate. When anyone knows enough factual data about another person it is relatively simple to request a replacement birth certificate from the Department of Vital Statistics, together with the five-dollar fee. With a birth certificate, anyone can then get a work ID, a school ID, or a check-cashing ID. With these in hand, a driver's license is the ultimate document.

Most driver's license examiners require a birth certificate imprinted with the state seal. After finding one who did not, I would edit the birth certificate by whiting out all unwanted data, making a blanked-out copy, filling in the blanks with the newly typed data, and then xeroxing a final copy of the reconstructed product.

Once a driver's license is issued, it is easy to travel in relative safety. As long as nobody knows otherwise, people have no reason to doubt the validity of the document

45

presented. I have opened checking accounts, financed cars, borrowed money, and secured a Master Card, all in the name of someone who really never existed. Because these false procedures for getting ID are now well known, it is not as easily done as in previous days.

My life as a fugitive was never easy, especially when just getting started after escape. Many times I had to survive on peanut butter and jelly sandwiches, sleep in the woods or in a car, and avoid all public contact until I could obtain new ID. At its worst, however, the life of a free fugitive seemed a thousand times better than the life of a caged convict. Until a man finds true freedom in obedience to the will of God, he is driven to the selfish freedom of a cunning animal. That was my experience and my life style until Christ gave me true freedom at a much later date.

CHAPTER 3

ON THE RUN
LIFE AS A YOUNG FUGITIVE

There are two things a fugitive must avoid while on the run: (1) old friends, especially those who are hustlers; and (2) family. I knew that such associations would put the police on my trail, yet I not only failed to avoid bad friends and family, but I sought them out, as if daring the police and begging for my own destruction. Every time I wandered more than two states away from my daughters in North Fork, thoughts of them seemed to draw me back. It was almost spring, and that season excited me with new hope and daring endeavors. My old friend, Sonny, masterminded my family reunions and covered my flanks during social activities.

In 1972 I was twenty–five, and my generation was making its mark in history with bold attitudes and activities of rebellion and wild hedonism. Drugs and raucous parties played an important part in this movement that often merged anti-establishment politics with anti-police resistance. In the spirit of such an era, I was able to rationalize my criminal behavior and feel very comfortable in this permissive habitat.

I found myself going to parties of ten to forty people, right in the middle of my old neighborhood. Sonny would first scout the scene to see if there were any known narcs or "blabber mouths." After a week or so of socializing, I would leave town like a sailor on leave. The police and Feds would hear that I had made the scene and begin shaking down the party goers, only to discover they had just missed me. It must have frustrated them terribly, which was exactly what I wanted. I was consumed by rebellion, false pride, and passive-aggressive hostility.

There were several close calls. I once attended a party where the police raided and arrested thirty-nine people. If a friend and I had not crawled through an upstairs rear window as they entered the front door below, there would have been forty-one arrested.

Another time, as I left Sonny's house thoroughly stoned, I decided to drive out to Beach County, ten miles away, to visit my sister. A narc who had been at Sonny's house and heard me say where I was going ducked out and notified the police. They knew exactly where to go, since they had raided her home just a few weeks earlier.

Sitting at a stop light, half stoned out of my head and listening to the stereo blast rock and roll music, I happened to notice in my rear view mirror several men running toward my car with drawn guns. If this had not been enough to make the hair stand up on my neck and drop the cheeseburger I was munching, the unmarked car that suddenly swerved in front of me was.

Since the car in front was too far to one side to fully block me, and the police were getting out with drawn guns, I floored the accelerator, pulling off the road around them. With loudly amplified singing of Joe Cocker and instrumental music of the *Mad Dogs and*

Englishmen, I could see only their lips moving. I felt sure their shouts definitely were not, "Good tidings of great joy."

Because all the police were out of their cars, I got the head start I needed to get away. After a few horrifying moments of daredevil driving in and out of Friday night traffic, and after several near collisions, I found myself on a deadend road with a bad tire. I parked the car on a crowded residential street, trying to make it appear that it belonged there.

I got out, locked the doors, and hid in some shrubbery between two houses. One lone police cruiser creeping up the street spotted the car; within seconds, the place was covered with more squad cars than I could count. From several blocks away I could hear the tires squealing as all units answered their radio calls and rushed to the scene.

I ran through yards, scaling fences, ducking or knocking down clothes lines, barely ahead of barking dogs and cursing cops. I felt like a wild boar caught in a hunters' foray. After five or six blocks I was completely sober. Everything I owned was in the car, so now I was in the same predicament as six months earlier when, after escape from Powhatan, I ran down the railroad tracks in the middle of the night, wondering where I was going and how I would get there. Needing some place to lie low until the heat wore off, I called the Wop. Just like a repeat of 1968, he put me in touch with Frenchy who, by then, had beat his case and was free.

I didn't know what Frenchy and Wop were doing, but I did know they had some crazy undercover police woman named Dina X. trying to trap them. They even seemed to recognize her schemes but passed them off as a joke. I never met her, never saw her, and never had anything to do with her; I definitely had nothing to do with her mysterious death several months later.

Frenchy carried me to Port City where I stayed with an old retired bootlegger and his family. They were strange people, but they took me in and treated me well. Their family included a young man named Junie. Through him I met his friend, Franky W., whose memory has brought me two decades of inner pain and remorse. I wish I had never met him, or rather, I wish he had never had the misfortune of meeting me.

Franky never lived to see the day he was old enough to legally drink in the bars. He was the greatest pool shark I've ever known, even though he was only nineteen years old. I went with Franky to different bars to back him up as he hustled other pool shooters. Old guys couldn't believe this young kid could whip them the way he did. I was always quite amazed myself.

I sincerely liked Franky and we formed a deep friendship. He looked up to me and shared many of his feelings with me. He was a sad kid who acted happy when he was high from smoking weed and drinking beer, just as I myself had so often done.

He told me the story of a real tough ex-convict who dated his sister and continually abused her. One day when Franky happened to witness him beating his sister, he picked up her gun and shot and killed her tormenter. He said his sister took the rap, claiming self-defense to spare him. I remembered the incident because I had once been in jail with the murdered man. I recognized his name and remembered his cruelty.

I admired Franky for defending his sister, but I also felt compassion for a sensitive, guilt-ridden kid who still had a hard time dealing with murder. His feelings of remorse seemed always eating at him, leaving him with perpetual melancholy. I never told Franky that I was on escape, but he knew from my ability to get him drugs and false ID that I was an accomplished hustler.

I knew Franky was burglarizing places with Junie and some others. I tried to warn him what he was getting himself into but contradicted my own counsel by helping him hit a place where he had previously gained entry but was unable to open the safe. It was a dumb spur-of-the-moment escapade that grew out of all-night drinking. Nearly blind drunk, we hit the place and got almost two thousand dollars. Franky thought he was rich, but the next day, with a sober mind, I knew I had made a bad mistake.

Although I didn't know him well, I realized that Franky could never endure police interrogation without telling everything he knew. And by example, I was encouraging him to get into the very thing that was already destroying my life. I was living proof of the old adage: *"Ill gotten gain is the beginning of great loss."*

At that time, however, I was spiritually blind. In my unregenerate confusion I honestly believed that society not only owed me the right to hustle but had in fact made me the hustler I was. I rationalized that none of my crimes was as bad as what I had endured from society's prisons and from self-righteous judges who allowed prosecutors to violate the law to obtain convictions of a young pauper unable to afford a good lawyer.

Despite my bitterness and "stinking thinking," I was not as bitter as many of the convicts and ex-convicts I have encountered. My family and my Catholic upbringing instilled a lingering flame of decency and fairness that was never totally extinguished.

After pulling off the score with Franky, I went to Florida with my friend Sonny. We always seemed to gravitate there, but this time we went to simply have fun. Upon arrival, I discovered that Sonny's old girl-friend, Anna, was living there and was the primary incentive for his going. She was the one who had talked Sonny into turning himself in back in 1968 when we were both on the run.

It was while a fugitive in Florida that I first learned something surprising about my personal appearance. I was quietly drinking in a Miami bar, minding my own business, when an inebriated lady of the night suddenly walked up, pointed her finger in my face, and exclaimed, "I know who you are!"

I was in absolute awe and wondered if she had already called the police. Should I make a dash for the exit or play it cool? As my curiosity outweighed my paranoia, I meekly inquired, "How do you know who I am?"

"By your looks, of course," she replied.

Then my confusion was further intensified by her explication: "I would know you anywhere; I have seen all your movies. And, incidentally, I want your autograph."

By now I was thoroughly perplexed. I then asked her, "How do I sign it?"

"Clint Eastwood of course!" she responded.

In just a matter of seconds, this unknown woman had stretched my emotions over paranoia, anxiety, desperation, panic, and finally relief. Numerous others since then have said I resemble Clint Eastwood, but none have caused such emotional trauma as that lady in Miami.

Soon thereafter I returned to Virginia. In April of 1972. I found a nice 1967 Chevrolet for eight-hundred dollars, obtained new ID, and headed back to Florida alone. I had met a girl there and wanted to see her again. With her I was able to forget my pain and feel that I had some value as a person. We both realized our relationship had no lasting basis, and I returned once again to Virginia.

Franky had become involved in more burglaries with several different people, some of whom I never knew personally but who were associates of my old associates. When Franky's girlfriend was caught with a bag of weed he had given her and the police pressured her, she began to tell them wild stories about Franky and "his gang." They devised a plan to get her to set up a score in hopes of infiltrating "the gang."

Some time later, the day before I was to head back to Florida, Frenchy got in touch with me to tell me he had a "dynamite score" lined up that was supposed to be good for fifty to sixty thousand dollars. The inside source was Franky's girlfriend; her mother supposedly worked there as a bookkeeper. Because her information was so vague I was suspicious, but Frenchy seemed to believe it.

After casing the site of her proposed hit, I immediately knew something was wrong. It was a motorcycle shop in a ratty neighborhood that appeared hardly able to survive, much less earn a profit. I was amazed that Frenchy could not see through such a phony setup, but he and Franky were completely fooled by the blarney of Franky's girl friend.

Wanting to know what was going on, I told them we should hit the place on the following night. I had Franky leave his tools, saying we needed to case it at night. We parked five blocks away and walked the rest of the way just before dark.

Since there was a vacant house on either side of the rear of the business, we ducked into the overgrown yard of one of them and settled comfortably in some bushes.

From our camouflaged position we observed the building at a distance of seventy yards.

Half an hour later, to our amazement, figures began to emerge from the shadows just two hundred feet away. They were carrying shot guns and heading toward the site of our proposed score, hiding themselves around the building. When several headed in our direction we quickly retreated without being observed.

I knew all along this score wasn't legitimate, and I had no intentions of hitting it, yet I wanted to know who was trying to betray me. I was convinced after our evening stakeout that Franky and Frenchy were both innocent; Franky's girlfriend was the traitor. But why would she sell us out? As I suddenly realized that Franky had told her all our exploits, I knew it was time for me to leave. I retreated to Beach County for the rest of the night.

The next morning Franky was arrested for attempted burglary of the motorcycle shop. He knew the alias I was using and the car I was driving; when the police finished with him he had provided all they wanted to know about me, both fact and fiction. A total of thirteen cops had staked the premises all night long. The next morning they informed the owner that burglars had attempted to break into his place but had somehow gotten away.

I was awakened that morning by my friend who told me I must contact another friend in North Fork who sent word for me to call him immediately. When I called my friend in North Fork he informed me that the whole Tri-City area was on special alert for me and my car. Since it is virtually impossible to leave Beach County and North Fork by auto except over the bridge or through the tunnel, and both were controlled by the state police, I went into hiding with friends in the West Ocean View area of

Tri-City. My friend Sonny arranged it, but, as is so often the case when too many people find out too much, someone informed.

Late one night, while I was going to my car to get clothes, no fewer than fifteen police, mostly from Port City, pounced on me, cuffed me, and began beating and kicking me without cause, without restraint, and without mercy. I believe to this day they would have killed me on the spot had it not been for one courageous policeman. Roy Boone, a North Fork uniformed officer who had grown up in my old neighborhood, pulled up on the scene and demanded that the detectives immediately stop. He then dragged my half-conscious body to his patrol car and put me in the back seat. One eye was swollen completely shut and I could hear nothing in one ear; the other ear was ringing so terribly it hardly worked. Blood flowed from my mouth and nose, and muscle cramps consumed my legs, hips and back where I had been kicked again and again and again. The pain in my testicles made me doubt that I could ever have children again.

They beat me with such venom that I unknowingly had a bowel movement in my pants. For weeks I had terrible body pains and for months my head throbbed. To this day, my hearing in one ear has never returned to normal. I had over three hundred dollars in my pocket and a Bulova Accutron watch on my wrist, all of which disappeared with the Port City police. This unprovoked beating was more brutal and more calculated than the notorious Rodney King beating by the Los Angeles Police two decades later.

All the way back to Port City a detective on either side of me would either elbow me or punch me in the side until I threw up, while they laughed. I never met any criminal in prison as cruel or vicious or sadistic as "Port City's Finest." Upon arrival at the jail, the photographer refused to even take my picture until someone cleaned the blood off my face.

Months later, three of these same policemen took the stand in court and perjured themselves under oath by declaring that they saw us try to pry open the back door of the motorcycle shop. One said it was me, another said it was Frenchy, and none could get their testimony to agree.

Many people in the courtroom believed that the prosecutor and the police twisted the truth from start to finish, but today people address that same prosetutor with deference as "Your Honor." He made his reputation by getting convictions any way he could, even when those convictions required suppressing the truth. He knew I had taken a polygraph test that proved my innocence conclusively, but because my polygraph might jeopardize his conviction record, he would not allow it to be reported. He convinced the judge to find me guilty in spite of the contradictions of police witnesses.

For years I have wondered how any judge would believe that three unarmed burglars could pry open a door while encircled by thirteen officers armed with shot guns, and then miraculously disappear unscathed. What I found even more incredible was that out of thirteen policemen, not a single one was willing to come forward with the truth. The unjust tactics of the prosecutor, the false testimony of thirteen policemen, and the obvious collusion of the judge produced a conviction and a sentence of three years.

Next I had a jury trial on another charge. Franky testified that the police and prosecutor told him what to say and how to say it, and that if he did not follow their directions he would get twenty years in prison where he would be raped, tormented, and maybe even killed. (These facts can be verified by reading the official court records.) The court ignored Franky's courageous testimony, found me guilty, and sentenced me to five years.

Frenchy was let out on bond. Junie and some other person I didn't even know were also out on bond. Stories in the newspaper portrayed a big-time burglary ring with me as the leader. During the next trial, a replica of the first, the jury deliberated only fifteen minutes before pronouncing me guilty. I had seven more trials pending when Franky failed to show up to testify; his body was discovered in the swamps of the Chesapeake. Just five miles away, authorities then found the skeletal remains of Dina X., the undercover police informant who was running with Frenchy, Wop, and dozens of other crooks against whom she was scheduled to testify.

By the time the newspapers embellished their lurid stories, there was hardly any truth I could recognize. A drug informant I had never met was killed somewhere in the city that same year and was also featured in a newspaper article that depicted me as a gangland mastermind. With my photo next to his, we were alleged to have been partners in leading an unholy ring.

A year later Frenchy was convicted of the murder of Franky W. and sentenced to life in prison. They never discovered how Dina X. died or who murdered her. For once I was thankful I was in jail when it happened. I was sent to the penitentiary in Richmond where I spent the next four years in maximum security.

I don't know how Franky died. To this day I am filled with profound sadness whenever I hear one of his favorite jukebox songs or see a sharp young pool shark. I have immeasurable regret for all the tragic things that happened to him, and for the part I played in his ruin. I feel tremendous empathy for his parents who must have gone through emotional torture over him. Franky was doomed from the day the Port City police devised their evil plan to entrap him. No matter which way he went, no matter what he did, he was doomed. In prison he would have died a different death. A young man saddled with the reputation the police had given him could never have survived mentally, even if he had survived physically. I have known several who survived physically only to take their own lives at a later time.

CHAPTER 4

HARD WORK AT LEGAL FREEDOM

BUT NO BRASS RING

My life has been repeatedly marked by events that were strange, unexpected, and unexplainable from a human perspective. This was the case in the fall of 1976, four years after the Port City episode. Together with three other inmates of the old state penitentiary in Richmond, I was caught in a steam tunnel below the prison compound where we had chiseled a hole through the cement wall of the tunnel and removed dirt to dig another tunnel.

We were all beaten, shot with stun guns and tear gas, and then locked up in solitary isolation of "C" building, a ghoulish prison within a prison. Two weeks later the Institutional Classification Committee placed us in indefinite segregation but failed to follow the proper procedure of writing up charges against us.

Penitentiary officials did not bother to charge us with attempted escape because they lacked evidence to prove such charges and because it was less trouble to ignore regulations. By merely labelling us "Suspected

Escape Risk," they could hold us in segregation for years without any evidence against us. If they charged us and were unable to prove their charges, they could not have held us in segregation. Such prolonged isolation was a fate worse than an additional year in prison. I was at their mercy, even though their actions violated regulations.

While consigned to segregation, an inmate not on "Padlock" could go to the courtyard for one hour of exercise twice each week under the watchful gaze of two gun towers thirty feet atop the walls. Even under such strict restraints I saw two men stabbed in their guarded courtyard.

To the amazement of everyone, the Parole Board, not knowing of my alleged attempted escape, granted me parole. The penitentiary authorities were now entrapped in a strange web of their own making. They dared not admit their duplicity to the Parole Board, yet they detested the thought that I was to be set free.

During this time I felt great excitement at the prospect of such a miraculous release, too good to be true. I also felt great fear, as suspicion mounted among my fellow convicts regarding what I had done to gain such undeserved parole. I didn't dare go on padlock, since this would feed their suspicions, yet it required great self-discipline to overcome my paranoia and walk out into the courtyard. I was particularly concerned about insinuations and threats made by "Tex," one of the three other apprehended "tunnel rats." He was a treacherous, weird character whose actions were unpredictable; I watched my back carefully during that six weeks prior to my scheduled departure.

On the day of my designated release, my sister, Miss Brooke, and her daughter, Ann, drove from Beach County to Richmond to take me home. The penitentiary authorities refused to release me, and my sister refused to accept their refusal. She demanded an audience with the warden, whereupon the guards bodily dragged her to the front gate for expulsion at the very moment the prison Catholic priest was entering. He demanded an explanation and was so outraged he immediately summoned an attorney friend of his, Tom Jones. Mr. Jones was a great lawyer and also a good man—a wonderful combination not regularly found.

After the lawyer informed the warden that he could not legally hold me without some kind of additional charge, the warden then quickly served a warrant on me for attempted escape. Since I had not yet been found guilty and there was no evidence that I had violated my parole, I was allowed to make bond on the charge, much to the chagrin of my captors.

Miss Brooke and Mr. Jones had pulled it off! As I walked out the gate I still expected the authorities to come up with another ploy just before 5:00 p.m., November 26, 1976. My sister and Ann were crying and giggling as I kept saying we had better get the heck out of there as quickly as possible before they could think up another excuse to put me back in.

My extreme anxiety was further intensified when my sister's Volkswagen bus would not start. Ann and I had to push it down the hill (thank God there was a hill!) while Sis popped the clutch. All this time we were all three glancing over our shoulders, waiting to see if the prison officials might be coming after us.

Since I was paroled to my parents' home in Glawstur, Virginia, my sister took me there. There the craziness began the first week I was home. Problems arose regarding the attempted escape charge: my dad and I resumed verbal conflict just like we had fifteen years earlier; worst of all, my parole officer seemed rather strange. When I saw how he badgered his own eight and nine year-old children and how he shaved their heads, I feared I might have trouble. I longed to maintain my precious freedom through societal conformity but had doubts about such future possibility.

I began driving ninety-mile round trips two or three nights a week to the "Thirsty Camel Bar" in West Ocean View, North Fork, to drink with my old friends. It seemed I always ran into my old friend, Sonny, and he was always more than willing to help my re-entry into society with lots of partying, wine, and women. I was completely drunk every time I drove the forty-five miles home. It still amazes me that I was pulled over and given a reckless driving ticket only once during that entire period.

I reported to my parole officer that I could no longer live in my father's house, since he and I simply could not get along, and he did not have enough work in his electrical business to keep me busy. My parents' home was too far from my children, and I wanted to build a relationship with them. I also explained that my sister had offered me a place in her home in Beach County and that I had a job offer in North Fork. After I gave him all the phone numbers, he checked them out and granted approval. He ordered me to report to the parole officer in Beach County and to tell the Beach County parole officer he would send written approval within a week.

I reported to the parole officer in Beach County, told him who I was, and explained my situation. He told me to report once each week until he received the paper work from Glawstur.

My sister Brooke had long ago divorced her first husband, Bob, and raised her two children, Robert and Ann, by herself. I don't know if Robert and Ann are more like my own kids or more like a brother and sister, but I love them dearly. They became a source of great encouragement to me as we enjoyed sharing the same house together. My sister had a lovely beach house in Beach County, on the Atlantic Ocean. My baby sister, Mary, also lived there, and my two younger brothers, Lawrence and Tucker, came on the weekends. We all enjoyed each other's company during some wonderful times that left many fond memories.

I was beginning to feel free and relaxed, even though the attempted escape charge in Richmond was still pending. I had to return there to see my lawyer and make court appearances about once each week. I finally received a jury trial, and, even though there was much circumstantial evidence, it was never proven that I was actually intending to escape. Unlike the Port City trials in 1972, the Richmond judge would not tolerate false reports and contradictions. The jury found me not guilty. It was a huge weight off my mind, but I felt more free than I really was; parole requirements still hung over my head like a guillotine.

Word spread that I was hanging out at the Thirsty Camel in North Fork, and this prompted a visit from two Richmond ex-cons. One of them, Lewis S., was one of the best outlaws I ever met, in so far as having moral character was concerned. He was loyal and dependable. The other ex-con, Bobby, however, had a serious drinking problem that often exceeded his self-control. When Lewis learned that I was financially stressed, he laid a thousand dollars on me. Since I had not requested his help, I was very surprised and very grateful. He was that kind of friend.

Although I had never pulled off any jobs with either of them, Bobby was after me to do a score with him. I always refused until one night when we were both drunk. I agreed, and we were soon rummaging around in search of burglary tools prior to hitting a department store in Beach County where Bobby had seen a safe. From the time we began drinking in the Thirsty Camel Bar until we landed in jail, the entire farce was like a slapstick comedy.

Because we needed a container of some sort to hold our tools, we stopped by my sister's house and picked up a green pillowcase. We somehow found our way to the store without having an accident and parked in a parking lot directly behind it, another dumb move. There were other cars in the lot belonging to customers of a restaurant-bar called *"The Jewish Mother,"* located beside the targeted store. The same alley that ran behind *The Jewish Mother* also ran behind the department store.

Bobby slung the pillowcase over his shoulder. With each of us thoroughly drunk and each holding a fresh beer in our hands, we strolled through the lot and into the alley. I climbed up on the roof and Bobby handed me the beers and pillowcase full of tools. Unfortunately, he handed it to me upside down, causing the crowbar, three-pound hammer, screw driver, punches, and chisels to fall, clanging down to the pavement. The crowbar hit Bobby on the head on the way down. Remarkably, no one heard us, or, if they did, they didn't do anything about it.

We finally retrieved the tools, but Bobby was too drunk to climb up. I had to go back down, help him up, and then climb back up again. This process was repeated twice, since we still had to ascend to a higher roof where we faced the windows of the upper story of the building. We sat and finished our beers before sawing out the steel window frame.

After removing the window, I suggested we leave for a while just in case we might have triggered an alarm or someone might have heard us. Bobby didn't want to do all that climbing again, so we argued for several minutes until I finally won him over. Meanwhile, the police were on their way in response to a silent alarm we had unknowingly activated.

Believing that nothing was amiss, we took our time getting down. We discovered our mistake when, coming out of the alley, we encountered what we thought was a beat cop who asked us what we were doing. We replied that we were just coming from the back entrance of the Jewish Mother. We were joined by half a dozen more police who put us in the back of a patrol car until they could investigate inside. After they checked the window, they carried us to jail. We were both released on bond the following day, sober and sorry.

In court the police falsified their report, claiming they saw us jump off the roof. I presume they thought it would strengthen their case and sound more exciting. Of course we were guilty, but the unwarranted prevarication and treachery of a few have always made it hard for me to trust any police officer until I know his moral character.

I was hardly in a position to complain about police lies, however, considering that my first response was to lie to my sister, denying the entire affair. She suddenly cut me off with a terse rebuff, declaring that she recognized her pillowcase from the evidence presented in court. I was caught like the cat who ate the canary, with feathers in my whiskers. I felt deeply ashamed, especially in light of all she had endured to obtain my freedom. Although slight of build and very much a lady, when wronged she has the capacity for tongue lashing worse than any physical punishment. I had betrayed and humiliated her. I too was deeply humiliated.

My humiliation led to the second resolution to get my life straightened out. And I really did try for awhile. I quit the bar scene, ignored calls from shady friends, and channelled my activities into hard work and visitation of my daughters.

About two weeks after my resolution I was arrested for parole violation. Since I had not yet been found guilty of the attempted burglary, they couldn't use that against me. Instead, they accused me of leaving my district without permission: to wit, moving from Glawstur to Beach County. At my parole revocation hearing the Glawstur parole officer claimed he had never approved any move to Beach County.

I was appalled that any state officer could give such a false report and still maintain any semblance of moral integrity. If that were true, why had I regularly reported to the Beach County parole officers? He had called my sister to ensure her willingness to take me in and had likewise called my employer to check my work performance. He previously told my mother, who does not lie for anyone (including me), that he gave me permission to move to Beach County. But at the hearing he claimed he had never granted any such permission.

I have often wondered what it is that leads people in authority to violate the truth. I think some believe they have a special dispensation to harass and eradicate individuals they consider unfit, using any means necessary, true or false, right or wrong, to do whatever they deem appropriate. I believe they often develop megalomania, believing that such ruthlessness pleases the public, that the public approves any means that produce the desired ends.

While I was in jail awaiting trial for attempted burglary, Bobby's wife came to visit and told me Bobby had been killed. In a bar drunk, he had threatened to hurt the wrong person, a man with a gun and drunk enough to use it. He shot Bobby in the head. The murderer was sentenced to only five years.

Bobby's tragedy was my third personal encounter with untimely death. It left me sad and depressed, fearing that I too was doomed to a life of misery and an early death by violence. I had been on parole for less than four months. Four months' freedom out of seven years' confinement didn't seem like very much, and it went by so fast that it hardly seemed real. I had failed to accomplish any of the constructive goals I had dreamed about during all those years in prison. Now I was going back for God only knew how long. All my sister's efforts seemed to have been in vain!

There were some Christians who came to the jail once or twice a week with a promise of divine power which enables believers to do things they otherwise could not do. I had known many opportunistic men in jails and prisons who "got religion" until they "got out," so I was very skeptical. But because I was also desperate to find meaning in life and to experience the power to change, I began to listen and participate in their Bible study. Why not? I didn't have anything else to do.

One Christian man, Wayne Skinner, took a special interest in me and invited me to attend services of a special ministry he had begun: "Outreach For Christ." He stated that God revealed to him that I too would someday participate in Outreach For Christ as a volunteer leader. I thought to myself his prophecy was crazy, but seventeen years later it has come to pass.

Things did begin to improve, including my attitude and the attitude of others toward me. One of the older jailers who had previously been a North Fork policeman and had chased me around when I was a kid took notice of my change in attitude and allowed me out of the cell block to help him do odd jobs around the jail, feeding inmates and washing laundry. I had never before done time like that, without animosity between my keepers and myself. It did make life in captivity much easier and more pleasant.

Janette, the daughter of one of the cooks in the kitchen, started coming to visit me. She was pretty and seemed to have a genuine interest in me. We became close. She had a little girl named Lenora, to whom I became quite attached. Years later I would see her often with great fondness. She was only four years old at the time and called me "Daddy Robert." She was very sweet and was starved for the love and affection she had never known from a real daddy.

With such improved relations, my lawyer was able to make a deal. Since I was going back to prison anyway, he was able to obtain a suspended sentence if I pled guilty; the prosecutor had a weak case and just wanted a conviction. Mr. Baker, the old jailer, and Wayne Skinner all went to bat for me, as did some of the other Christians. So, after being in jail for over a year, I was finally sent back to prison.

I kept my "new attitude" and eventually, to everyone's amazement, made trusty. Even so, it was only after four and a half years of hard time that I again made parole. Furthermore, it happened only after my family hired an expensive, prestigious lawyer who had clout and connections. Mercy and justice were not dispensed until the skids were greased by the power of money.

In January 1981 I was again released, a stranger in a strange land. With the exception of four months' parole and my short-lived escapes, I had served twelve consecutive years. Before that, I had served my first term of fifteen months. I was thoroughly institutionalized, afflicted with a mentality beyond the comprehension of normal people who have never done time in prison.

In prison, bells and whistles dictate all daily activity, and paranoia is a condition of life: always on your guard, always struggling for your place of respect, always second guessing what others think of you and want from you. You are always gaming, whether smuggling a steak sandwich from the mess hall or stealing a decent pair of boots from the store room. In prison everyone knows what you are, or at least what you are about. Consequently, you don't have to hide anything from people whose conversations usually center on some aspect of crime. It is truly a different world which functions according to a different mind-set.

Being free after so long produced a new trauma all its own. No longer having to worry about someone stabbing me in the back while asleep or in the chow line, I suddenly had new worries: how to handle responsibilities requiring personal initiative; how to hide a past; how to keep up with the fast pace of civilian life. Dealing with such trauma seemed overwhelming.

Whereas survival in prison demanded the cunning of a fox combined with the conformity of a robot, survival on the outside demanded the responsibility and initiative of a self-disciplined individualist. What a shocking transition, this 180-degree immediate change of direction!

My paranoia caused me to fear serious conversation with anyone on the outside, as I struggled to remember and fulfill my new responsibilities. And because everything seemed to take twice as long as anticipated, I was constantly late. I found that I easily became frustrated, although I managed to keep it suppressed. I was afraid of my emotions. And without anyone to confide in, all this traumatic transition intensified the isolation. There was hardly a soul anywhere on the streets I could relate to.

During this time of isolation, my old friend, Sonny, paid me a visit. I was overjoyed to see him. We went off together to some of the old haunts to have a few drinks and check out the girls. I must have talked his ears off. At last, I could finally unburden myself to someone I knew I could trust, someone willing to listen and understand. His presence was truly refreshing to me.

I did have one problem that caused me concern: someone somewhere had obtained my ID and was using it. I discovered it six months prior to parole, when an investigator from the Department of Motor Vehicles came to see me. Because I had become a state-wide trusty, the State Department Of Corrections had allowed me to regain my driver's license, and the Department of Motor Vehicles received applications from two men named Robert C. Witt. Each had the same date of birth and same Social Security number; only the addresses were different. The investigator wanted to know if I recognized the other signature. I did not.

I mentioned it to Sonny because I knew that only someone from our old neighborhood could know all that information about me. At first he denied knowing anything about it, but on our way to get drunk several months later, Sonny confessed that he had given the ID I left at his house to a guy on the run, Terry T., the same unscrupulous character who had caused me trouble back in 1967. Sonny swore that Terry would never again use it. He would either destroy it or get it back to me.

Unknown to me, the police began casing my previous address in Beach County, looking for the truck described by my parole officer. Because I didn't live there anymore, the truck was never seen, and the police reported to my parole officer that I didn't appear to live there. They didn't tell the parole officer which house they were checking until after I had my sister and others call to verify that I was home every week night and most weekends. Then the police recognized the obvious: They had the wrong address.

I had a good job, working in my trade as an electrician. Several times after leaving work I noticed detectives parked in nearby cars, obviously checking on me. To complicate matters, Terry was arrested while using my ID. After he was released on bond and arrested a second time with my ID, he assaulted the arresting officer and ran. By this time my parole officer was ready to send me back to prison and had in fact put out a warrant for my arrest. That was in addition to the warrant in North Fork for assaulting a police officer.

Two parole officers came out to my job site to tell me there was a warrant for my arrest. Only after my lawyer and I confronted the assaulted officer did we prove it wasn't me. It almost cost me my job, and it riled my parole officer so badly I had to report to her weekly for three months. It also scared me, especially when it happened yet a third time before Terry finally quit using my ID. If I had not had concrete evidence of my whereabouts at the time of the assault, I would have been on my way back to prison immediately. Fortunately, I was able to withstand the pressure and outlast the confusion during those turbulent days.

In 1984, with a ten-thousand-dollar loan from my brother, I started my own electrical contracting business. The business employed a staff of three to twelve workers and grossed $200,000 the third year in business, yet it never made a profit. As my brother once said, "You are a good electrician but a poor manager." I tried very hard to make it succeed. It was quite common for me to work sixteen hours per day, six and seven days per week.

The year before I went into business I went to a party of a friend of my brother and met a young lady I will call Martha (to protect her from the pain that would result from revealing her true name). She was the supervisor of the girl honored at the party. Martha and I talked during the entire party, and the next day she invited me to her house in the country. I liked and admired her very much, and I was impressed with the lifestyle she had established out in her country home.

I remember telling my sister that I had met "Miss Perfect." She was the type of girl I knew my family would be crazy about, but I felt she would probably reject me if she knew my sordid past. I did not realize then that I was using the wrong qualities of assessment in looking for a potential mate. After she began to show an interest in me, I knew I had to let her know who I really was, to spare her future embarrassment.

I called and asked her to meet me at a certain restaurant in Beach County. I told her as briefly as possible of my past, that I was not only an ex-convict but was presently on parole. To say she was shocked is putting it mildly. She listened attentively, eyes growing wider as I proceeded. She thanked me for being honest and frankly told me she would have to think about it.

I went home thinking we were through, but she later called and invited me to her house for dinner. She informed me that she respected my honesty but never again wanted to hear about my criminal past, nor would her family and friends ever find out, if at all possible. I agreed to her conditions, and we began dating.

A year or so later I began to feel it would not work out, and I attempted to ease out of the relationship. This seemed to hurt Martha, and I felt guilty that she was hurt. She seemed to care for me and wanted our relationship to become permanent. I finally decided that if someone wanted me that much I had better hang on to her. As it turned out, Martha would have been much better off if I had followed my initial instincts and ended the relationship at that time. Instead, we proceeded to have a big wedding with all her family and all my family involved.

Martha tried desperately to re-mold me, yet she didn't want me to have anything to do with the re-molding process. I always had the feeling that she didn't really trust me or have faith in me; my past was strictly taboo, a forbidden topic. Even though she was a fine person and a dutiful wife, I felt frustrated in pretending to be something I really wasn't; I could never relax and truly be myself with her.

Eventually ex-convicts began to look me up after word in the prison grapevine spread that Witt was now a very successful businessman, rolling in dough. Cons like to have influential friends for various reasons. Those who are genuine friends appreciate the success of a colleague to disprove the common belief that, "Convicts cannot change: once a hustler, always a hustler; once an outlaw, always an outlaw."

Everyone seemed under the illusion that I was a success, doing well financially, and that brought a conniving individual into my life in the fall of 1985. Many convicts like to find ex-cons who are doing well and then mooch off them. Such was the case with several who came to see me, but none quite so brazen as Robert "Ox" Skidmore. Even before he was released, he got my phone number from a friend, Aubry "Pork Chop" S., and called to ask if I would give his son a job. I did. His son, Bobby, turned out to be a good man and one of my best workers.

Later, Ox called me again, asking if I would write the Parole Board a letter promising to give him a job. I did. After he made parole, he was at my shop the next day, and, after departure of everyone else, we sat around the shop exchanging stories about people we knew, reminiscing about things we had been through in prison. It was pleasant to talk about it with someone, but I sure wish that someone had been someone other than Ox Skidmore.

Ox kept coming around borrowing money and wanting company. Even though I was always extremely busy, I made time for him. He continually talked about going after a score, and, even though he was a safe man himself, he wanted to know everything I knew about cracking safes. I tried to make it clear to him that I had retired from burglary and hustling.

He came to me one night all excited about a score he had found. He said he needed my help and I refused. Several days later he caught me when I was depressed and in desperate need of money. Much to my regret, I gave in to temptation.

We hit the place and stole almost three thousand dollars. He later accused me of cheating him and demanded that after the next score we would strip when we split the money. I emphatically told him that there would not be another score, not with me anyhow. I ordered him to get out of my life.

I felt deep regret and remorse for having gone back into this sort of thing. I was having enough problems with my business, my marriage, and my emotional instability; now I had made it all even worse. I felt absolutely ill for having allowed myself to revert to crime with a person like Ox. I had begun to assess his sociopathic actions even before we hit that score. He had no morals, no scruples, and was willing to do anything to anybody for money.

When I received telephone calls at home from "old friends," Martha complained and nagged me until I changed the phone number. When Sonny needed help, Martha went into a rage. She never realized that, with all his faults, Sonny was still my lifelong friend; he had always been there for me when no one else was.

In addition to everything else, I was having a grave problem with my older daughter, dating a young man who was causing us grief at the very time my business was wearing me down. Anxiety over debts resulted in an ulcerated stomach, and I often woke up during the night, terrified as to how I would come up with two thousand dollars by 2:00 p.m. to meet the day's obligations. I became expert at robbing Peter to pay Paul, but it only led me deeper and deeper in debt. I never realized a business could require such hard work, generate so much debt, and provide such intense stress with no joy.

I learned from experience that accurate bookkeeping is the key to business success, without which the owner can neither plan nor manage effectively. I also learned that employees make you or break you. Undisciplined workers are like wayward children; they cause great heartache and create havoc. I haphazardly hired an incompetent estimator who cost me over fifty thousand dollars. Trying to be a nice guy to my employees cost me terribly. I knew nothing about running a business, with no schooling and no managerial experience. My years in prison taught me irresponsibility and little else.

The business wasn't the only thing driving me crazy. Martha was continually angry because of the long hours I worked and her perception that I placed my friends and my daughter ahead of her. My daughter was equally angry because she felt I put Martha ahead of her. Sonny was angry because Martha didn't like him; he felt I wasn't doing enough for him. Then there were all those ex-convict friends who continually wanted me to do something for them or commit crimes with them. I felt pressed on all sides by everybody, sucked dry emotionally as well as financially.

The greatest torment of all was Ox Skidmore. Even though Martha, Sonny, and my daughter caused me stress, they still cared about me. Ox, on the other hand, ignored my wishes and actually recruited my most trusted friends to betray me and do his bidding. Some of them called and told me what he was doing. He was the kind of thief who did nothing by himself and always wanted someone else to do his dirty work, a con artist in the truest sense of the word. Initially, I thought he was rather dumb; I believed that I was smart enough to spot and handle devious con artists. That's how shrewd he was: dumb like a fox!

Ox went to see one of my friends in Richmond, Lewis S., who was honestly trying to make a new life for himself, working every day to be a productive law-abiding citizen. Then Ox brought him to North Fork to see me. When he left us for a few minutes alone, Lewis told me that Ox wanted him to convince me to do a score. I told Lewis I wanted nothing to do with any more crime, and he dropped it. Lewis always respected my feelings, as I did his.

On the trip back to Richmond, Ox convinced Lewis to go on a certain score by promising him twenty to thirty thousand dollars. The temptation was too great for Lewis. Several weeks later, they hit the house that had been rejected by every other hustler Ox had approached. Lewis, like me when I was hustling, didn't burglarize houses; it was too much of an invasion of personal privacy, poking around in another man's castle, looking for his family valuables, usually uninsured. But Ox had no such scruples and would steal anything from anybody, any time, anywhere he could.

Years later, when my lawyers gained access to court records, we learned that Ox had proposed hitting a credit union the FBI had been investigating with great zeal. An FBI informant named Brad, a sometime associate of Ox, told the Feds he heard him talking about the credit union job. When the Feds instructed Brad to tell Ox about this house job, he set the whole thing up by saying that the bookie living there was a country and western music enthusiast. Ox proposed sending him and his wife free tickets to a country and western concert at a local colosseum, thus leaving the bookie's vacant house an easy target for burglary.

The Feds, in turn, told the Beach County SWAT team that one of their reliable informants told them of a house job to be pulled off by two armed, dangerous safe crackers. The Feds wanted to catch one of the credit union burglars in order to force him to help solve that crime and other credit union cases.

After Ox convinced Lewis his financial happiness would come from this house score, they sent the concert tickets for the night of the scheduled hit. When Ox and

Lewis entered the back door of the house, they were greeted by a dozen armed members of the police SWAT team.

The next morning at work my secretary, Lori, told me Ox was on the phone. I told her to tell him I wasn't in. A few minutes later the phone rang again, but this time it was Dean, Ox's other son. Dean said that his dad said I had better get him out on bond. I told Dean I wanted nothing to do with his dad. An hour later he called again to tell me his dad said to tell me that Lewis S. was also in jail with him.

I went down to get Lewis out on bond. Because Lewis was from Richmond, the bondsman refused to get him out without Ox. So I ended up spending $1,600 of company money to spring both of them. Lewis ended up getting three years for the house burglary. Ox, as per agreement with the Feds and the Beach County prosecuting attorney, was never tried. Years later I obtained a copy of the court records revealing how he was granted total immunity.

For the next six months Ox kept hounding me, literally "bugging" me, as I discovered years later. He was so intrusive and so obnoxious I even changed my work phone numbers. He then kept coming to the shop, even after I told him to leave, trying to get me to describe how I had broken into sophisticated safes, or neutralized alarm systems. Everything I said was being recorded by Federal agents at the other end of the body microphone hidden under Ox's clothing.

By this time my marriage had deteriorated to such a point that I dreaded going home at night. I started sleeping on a cot in the back of the shop. I didn't want to see or talk to any ex-cons, especially not Ox Skidmore! Just the thought of him made my stomach turn. He was about sixteen years older than I, and, even though I had never known him in prison, we had numerous mutual friends. All those old convict friends described him as totally bad, and when other convicts speak totally bad about one of their own it truly indicates the lowest depths. About the time Ox made parole, his son, Bobby, went home from work one day and shot and killed his neighbor for beating up his kid brother, Dean. No one shoots anyone else six times in front of ten witnesses unless he is emotionally out of control. It had been an ongoing feud, and even though Bobby had repeatedly requested police intervention, it was never given.

Because I had talked to him on the phone a few minutes before the incident and was aware of the situation, Bobby subpoenaed me as a witness. In court, Ox showed me a wad of hundred dollar bills that totaled over ten grand and said he had five times more than that stashed away. It infuriated me that Bobby had an inexperienced court-appointed lawyer who was doing nothing for him while his own father brandished all that money. Ox could have hired his son the best lawyer available, but would not. That very day Ox told me he was going to hire a sharp lawyer to get an old stealing partner out of prison, while he watched his own son thrown to the wolves. He also failed to repay any of the money he owed me, but I didn't care; I just wanted him out of my life.

During that time everything suddenly seemed to be falling apart. Sonny's mother, Reba, became very ill. She was a wonderful woman and I thought the world of her. She and I had had many talks together over the years. When Sonny was out of town I often went to the store for her or dropped in just to say hello. Her daughters also checked on her, but often she was alone. Reba had been losing an ongoing battle with cancer for a long time. Finally, it became so serious she was hospitalized.

I took time out from my busy schedule to see her and comfort Sonny in the midst of his grief. Because he had injured his back and could not work, he was drowning himself in booze. His mother's suffering was mercifully cut short by death, and I was honored to be a pallbearer at her funeral. It changed my life forever.

That change came in the form of Elizabeth Dunn Kabler, who stood facing me across the grave while someone recited a poem reminiscent of Reba's life and death. I did not hear the words of the eulogy, so intent was my fascination with this beautiful young lady. As she affectionately leaned against her Uncle Sonny, I seemed to see little sparkles of sunlight dancing all around her.

The more I fastened my eyes on her, the more I had a strange feeling I had seen her before. It gradually dawned on me that I had had this same feeling three years earlier, and the source was the same. Betsy looked different now, a little more mature. Perhaps it was the sadness of the moment, or perhaps she was even more beautiful than before, but I was just as smitten at Reba's funeral as when I had seen Betsy the first time at Reba's Christmas party, three years earlier.

I remembered dancing with her during that Christmas party. I also recalled that she seemed unimpressed with me, causing me to conclude that it was out of order to pursue any attachment to her. At that time she was only nineteen, was going to college in Florida, was the pride of her wealthy stepfather, and must have had many better prospects than an ex-convict with an abominable past and a dubious future.

In addition, I was then escorting my girlfriend at the Christmas party, subsequently my wife, Martha. Three years later, at Reba's funeral, I was encountering the same kind of frustration, plagued by a wrecked marriage that began and died between the two breath-taking appearances of Betsy.

After the graveside service, I felt that I had to approach her. We almost ran to each other, whereupon I took her hands in mine, expressed my sorrow about her grandmother, and almost involuntarily blurted out that she was even more beautiful than I had remembered her being three years earlier. The look in her eyes was dazzling, as if I were some lost love from years gone by.

"Where was it I saw you last?" she asked with peculiar interest. I reminded her of the Christmas party, unable to discern whether or not she remembered me. My heart leaped when she said she hoped I would attend the wake at Sonny's house with friends and family. The wake turned out to be more like a party, which was just the way Reba would have wanted it.

Initially, there was an air of sadness as people filed in from the funeral, but they soon began to socialize in the relaxed spirit of another one of Reba's parties. Much to my delight, I kept finding myself face to face with Betsy. Surprisingly, I didn't feel constricted that I was still legally married, or that she had a fiance in Florida, or that she was Sonny's niece. For the moment, I just wanted to enjoy her company, and I refused to think about anything that might interfere with it.

Betsy seemed to do and say little things that revealed a personal interest in me, but I passed it off as an overactive imagination on my part. There were several other men, younger and better looking, who were after her. I could hardly stand the thought of others drooling over so beautiful and precious a soul.

Late that night, after almost everyone was gone, I realized it was past time for me to leave. I was paying my farewell respects when Betsy took my breath away by whispering, "Please don't go." Although it was several days before I told her, I was deeply in love with her at that very moment.

I may never stop paying, in one way or another, for my infidelity while still legally married. My first wife left me and remarried while I was still in prison; I couldn't change that. But this time it was different. Even though my second marriage was falling apart, I still had no excuse. My biggest domestic mistake was marrying Martha for the wrong reasons. That is why I always advise others to be very careful before "tying the knot." Marriage should be a lifelong commitment, entered into with clear definition of goals and expectations. No one should ever marry out of a sense of obligation or for selfish gain or with hidden agendas.

Martha married me because she wanted security, and I married her because I thought she was the kind of girl I needed to reorder my life. These were the wrong reasons, and the absence of romance and nurture eroded our dull relationship. I didn't trust her, she didn't trust me, and we both became selfish and resentful in our attitudes toward each other. And God was never a part of the marriage. I'm not even sure how I felt about God back then.

One thing was certain: Betsy did not break up my marriage with Martha; it was already dead when we met at the funeral. Nevertheless, I will always regret that we began our relationship prematurely, on unholy ground, so to speak. I also deeply regret the pain I caused Martha. She would have been better off if we had walked away from each other instead of getting married. I sincerely hope she has found happiness since then.

I stayed so late at Sonny's house after the wake I ended up spending the night. My first waking thought was of Betsy. I hoped she was still there, for I wanted to see her and talk to her again. I wanted to determine if the things she said and the way she acted toward me the previous night had resulted primarily from drinking and the momentary emotions of the event. As I was leaving to go to work, I was elated when she hugged me good-bye and said she hoped to see me again real soon. I thought to myself: *You sure will!*

I went through that day's chores at work with a mild hangover, dodging and ducking all my problems and responsibilities as best I could. There were several phone calls from Martha, and that made me cringe. After so many various calls from people, I finally told Lori I could not face any more problems that day.

Lori was one of the finest people I have ever had the privilege of knowing. She was a great secretary to me, she was a good wife to her husband, a wonderful mother to her kids, and a very understanding and compassionate person. If anyone on this earth knew what I was going through at that time, it was Lori. She always tried to help me in every way possible, yet without being intrusive. I am sure I often overburdened her. There were times when I put Circuit Electric Company completely in her lap and just left.

On the evening after the funeral, I found myself anxious to finish the work day so I could try to go visit Betsy. I kept wondering if she would still be there or if she really wanted to see me again. I had heard her say she was going to be around for a few weeks before going back to Florida.

I did see her that evening, thus beginning the most awesome romance imaginable. We spent many long hours together, talking, laughing, and crying. I poured out my heart to her, sharing things I had never told anyone else, and she spilled her heart to me. She comforted my weary soul like a mother comforts her child, and she loved me with that love I had always hungered for. The many obstacles we both faced were momentous, yet paled into insignificance compared to the unthinkable possibility of losing each other.

It is hard to believe that something as wonderful as the magic of those July weeks of 1986 could produce added turmoil in my life, but it did. I had to make a decision about my marriage. Martha would not accept a divorce and was extremely emotional about such a prospect. I felt as though I was destroying her, yet at the same time, I never believed she even liked me, much less loved me.

Meanwhile, Betsy was feeling very uncomfortable about seeing a married man, and at one point even suggested we should cease seeing each other until I had finalized a divorce. The second day we were together she had asked me about my marriage, soon after her uncle warned her that I was married. I honestly told her I was miserably married, but I wasn't totally honest when I told her I was separated. She discovered this before returning to Florida.

Now I was miserable on every front, as were both Martha and Betsy. Betsy was going through the exact same thing with her fiance, so she couldn't be too judgmental with me. The complexity of it all seemed crazy. I would have a heart-rending encounter with Martha, and within an hour have a heart-breaking encounter with Betsy when she found out I had talked to Martha.

I was tempted more than once to flee so far away I would have no contact with anyone. But, in addition to all the interpersonal trauma, there were still the problems of Circuit Electric Company; the business was dragging me down worse than a ball and chain. And all the ex-convicts kept showing up.

I started drinking a lot and smoking weed to escape the pressure of all my problems. I would seek out a lonely stretch of beach or a path through the woods in solitude. Loneliness, in turn, caused me to yearn for Betsy all the more.

One day, when my longing for Betsy seemed intolerable, I decided to fly to Florida to see her. We spent three wonderful days together. Each day I called Lori and gave her instructions regarding Circuit Electric Company. After that first Florida trip, I flew or drove back to see Betsy every two or three weeks.

On the one hand, each trip was exhilarating and relaxing while there; on the other hand, it increased stress afterward, as my credit card accounts were all overextended. It was like living on a seesaw, with the ups higher, the downs lower, and the alternations more rapid. Something had to be done! I finally realized I had to leave Martha and close Circuit Electric Company.

Wise decision making is one of the marks of maturity and often requires bluntness for the good of all concerned. It seems paradoxical, but a mature man can be both brutally frank yet gentle at the same time. This is the essence of his God-given role as a compassionate leader who makes right decisions. I was over forty years old before I learned this important truth.

Many times when I thought I was being nice I was actually cowering from my responsibilities and ultimately causing many people grief, including myself. I now realize that my lack of courage in making hard decisions caused me to choose bad company and do the wrong things, including criminal activities. I personally believe that mature honesty, wisdom, and inner strength are impossible without the power of God, since He is the grand Architect of true manhood.

Closing Circuit Electric Company was my one sound decision during that chaotic period, finally admitting that I was a miserable failure in business and ending the insane downward spiral of debt and disorder. Closing a business, however, is much more difficult than opening one. There were jobs to be completed, bills to be paid, receivables to be collected, and unpaid taxes to be settled. Worst of all, I had to face my brother, an investor and part owner in the business.

I had extended credit too easily and had incurred thousands of dollars of receivables I could not collect. I finally gave him all our mobile radios and some other assets in lieu of his investment. I sold tools, trucks and office equipment to pay bills. Neither he nor anyone else will ever know the real debt I incurred in that business. I juggled, begged, and borrowed large sums of money, channeling it through other jobs to pay the bills.

I went to Florida, picked up Betsy with all her belongings, and came back to Virginia in a U-Haul truck. We rented her mother's vacant condo in Beach County and tried to settle into a normal life. We began to work out our problems and overcome our obstacles. No one had my new phone number or knew where I was staying, and since the shop was closed half the time, no one could find me. That was the way I wanted it; I was in hiding. For the first time in years, I was able to relax, appreciate life, and enjoy the love of my wonderful sweetheart.

Betsy took all the money she had in the bank and I took all the money I could raise and we placed a five thousand dollar down payment on a piece of property in Northern Virginia, out in the country on the Rappahannock River. We also found an apartment in nearby Fredricksburg, and potential jobs for each of us. After all we had been through, we were ready to start a new and exciting life together, confident we could handle anything that lay ahead.

I was so relieved to be getting away from past mistakes and residual stress that I felt I had a new lease on life. I felt in my heart that I had learned much about life and about myself. I believed that with Betsy our dreams could be realized, and that I could still be a law-abiding, fulfilled person.

We had approximately one week of unfinished business and responsibilities to clear up and we both looked forward to getting it all out of the way. We were anxious to begin our new life in the country and escape the unpleasant past, with all the undesirable people in it.

On September 23, 1987, after completing the final financial report and listing all our receivables, I headed out to see my brother and officially close Circuit Electric Co., Inc. I was in a hurry to complete the close-out and then meet Betsy at the condo where she had packed things we would carry up to Fredricksburg that evening. I was excited.

I locked the shop, got in my car, and drove in the direction of my brother's office. Suddenly a car pulled sideways into the path of my car, whereupon I slammed on the brakes. Five or six other cars immediately surrounded me, as detectives and FBI agents jumped from their vehicles, pointing pistols and shotguns at my head. Screaming all kinds of things, they told me they were the police, and commanded me to put my hands on top of my head. I remember thinking to myself, "My God, what's happening? What do they think I've done? This isn't the normal way to be arrested!"

Their shouts still echo in my head to this day: *Mr. Witt, you are under arrest for the February 1986 burglary of the Port City Naval Credit Union and the grand larceny of $192,000!* Memories of that terrible encounter continued to interrupt my sleep for many years thereafter.

CHAPTER 5

BACK ON THE RUN AS A SEASONED FUGITIVE

I kept wondering if my inquisitors were only trying to scare me, or if they really thought I was the culprit and were on a "fishing expedition" to gain facts they didn't already know. All signs pointed to the latter. They left me alone in the interrogation room, scared stiff, and waited about twenty minutes before coming back to add more pressure, putting the squeeze on a little tighter.

"Your bond is $260,000, Witt. You won't see daylight for a long time, but if you cooperate we can do something about that high bond."

"I want a lawyer," I replied.

"You know, Witt, the Feds have got enough evidence to hang your butt. We don't need your help; we just want to help you help yourself." I knew from experience just how anxious they were to help me or any other ex-convict. They wanted to help me put myself right into a terrible trick.

"I want a lawyer!" The situation was scary, but I was more angered than scared by their tactics.

Then they left me alone again, only to return fifteen or twenty minutes later with the same line. They finally carried me to jail and told the desk sergeant, "We've got you a tough customer here. Put him where you put the rest of the tough guys."

"We've got a place for him," the jailer replied with a cynical grin; and he did. It was a six-man cell adjoining a block with five other cells, each with a toilet and a bed. The block itself was about twenty feet long and perhaps four feet wide, with metal benches welded to the bars and a shower and toilet at the end. My cell already had seven men, one of whom laid his mattress on the floor, as I also had to do. But during the day we couldn't keep our mattresses there because the men from the six cells wandered up and down the narrow floor, taking a shower, watching TV, playing cards, or just moving about.

There was a telephone on a cement column available for collect calls only during the day; at night it was cut off. Around midnight they rolled the six cell doors shut from controls outside the block. My end of the floor stayed wet and mirky. I also discovered during the night that there were bed bugs. Several bit me, making sleep very difficult.

I was sick, really sick, both mentally and physically. I had diarrhea for two days. I was going "cold turkey" from freedom, comfort, and love to captivity, misery and hate. People in jail act like they hate everything and everybody, and many of them aren't acting. Any man who is tried, condemned in court, and sent to jail feels hatred. It took great self-discipline to avoid surrendering self-control to such hatred. As I slowly overcame the hatred, I was able to think more clearly and fit the pieces together.

I was charged with burglary of three businesses, two of which I had never even heard of; the third was the Naval Yard Federal Credit Union in Port City. On February 6, 1986, the credit union safe had been robbed of $192,000, and then, September 18, 1987, a year and a half later, I was accused of the heist. I remembered that my electrical company twice had done some work for the Navy Yard Credit Union. I distinctly remembered because they were delinquent in paying their bill. My company also performed electrical work at the home of the manager of the credit union in 1984 or 1985.

I began to recall other things about that particular credit union: Ox Skidmore had asked me about the place and said his son told him that when he did a job there as one of my employees he saw all kinds of money. His son, Bobby, had been on that job as an electrician's helper.

After a few phone calls I began to piece the puzzle together. Ox Skidmore had bargained his way out of a conviction in the Beach County home burglary by fingering me as the one who did the credit union job. He told them some far-fetched tales to escape prosecution for two burglaries and his aggravated parole violation. Much later I discovered just how much freedom he parlayed with his colorful fabrications about me. Federal agents not only convinced prosecutors in two different cities to drop all charges, they even persuaded the Virginia Parole Board to free him.

I could not understand how the prosecuting attorneys could dismiss punishment of such blatant, repeated criminal behavior in order to entrap a man whose crimes were less serious. The police did not have a single shred of evidence against me apart from the self-serving testimony of Ox Skidmore. They seemed so determined to convict me they would do anything and ignore legal ethics.

91

Somehow in my misery I was able to think of other things. It was obvious I wasn't getting out, just like they promised. The day after I was arrested, a lawyer told me that no judge would touch my bond. I discovered that the 1972 murder of Frankie, my friendly witness, came back to haunt me again. The prosecutors and police told the judge that if I were released I would now be a threat to this witness, Ox Skidmore, as I previously had been to Franky. This was preposterous, since I was in jail when Franky was killed; even if I had masterminded his murder from a jail cell at that time, why could I not do it again?

However, I never got a chance to argue this or anything else in my favor because the authorities refused to grant me a hearing as guaranteed in legal due process. This refusal of the court to follow Constitutional due process requirements gave me a terrible feeling of doom.

After thorough assessment of the situation, I concluded that escape was my only hope. I began to sharpen my senses to every possible weak spot. Because I felt doomed no matter what I did, I decided I might as well go for broke.

I now felt sure that Martha would quickly proceed with divorce. But how long would Betsy wait? Betsy was a beautiful woman who had become the center of my world. My heart began to ache for her as I was overwhelmed with a sense of desperation. I struggled to cope with doubt and depression.

When I called Betsy she was very upset, but vowed to stand beside me. I discussed with her all the immediate obligations I could remember; I gave her names and telephone numbers and a list of errands to do for me and the business. She relayed my instructions to the only remaining employee, Matt, as to how he should finish the remaining two jobs we had promised. She paid bills and collected money from clients. Betsy's worst errand was having to go to my brother's office for his signature on dissolution papers and to tell him all that had happened.

Even in the midst of our trauma, I realized it would have been an even worse nightmare if it had happened two months earlier when I had several people on the payroll and owed the bank even larger sums of money. Although I was then oblivious to His leading, I now realize that God did grant this mercy in His timing.

Meanwhile, I had befriended a young man in the cell block with me. He was about the only friendly face in the entire jail and the only other white prisoner. He let me leave my mattress and personal belongings in his cell during the day, and allowed me to use his toilet and sink. I was shocked to learn that Wilbur had been jailed for simply defrauding an innkeeper. He had failed to pay his motel bill of $260.

Prior to that time I had never heard of any authorities mixing misdemeanors and felons together in jail. I knew it violated State Department of Corrections guidelines, but this jail seemed to be so freewheeling they did whatever they pleased, regardless of state laws or correctional guidelines. Guards ignored inmate pleas for any type of help and refused to enter the cell block unless there appeared a possibility of death, and maybe not even then.

The guards acted like they also hated being there, and I could hardly blame them; it was about the noisiest, hottest jail I had ever occupied up to that time in my life. When guards did enter the cell block, inmates screamed at them and cursed them. It was so noisy that anyone making a telephone call had to scream into the mouthpiece while trying to plug the other ear. The guards' contempt for and lack of recognition of their prisoners ultimately proved very helpful in my escape.

I developed a genuine appreciation of Wilbur and decided to pay his motel bill. I called Betsy and added that to her list of things to do. She and I had just borrowed $3,000 from the bank several days before my arrest and planned to use it to pay outstanding bills and finance our move to Northern Virginia. I told Betsy to get a signed receipt when she paid the innkeeper and convince him to drop the charges against Wilbur. Wilbur then suggested that I take his place and walk out when his release was ordered.

In response to Wilbur's suggestions, I began to ponder such a possibility. If I took Wilbur's place in court, the innkeeper would recognize me as an imposter, so that would not work. I decided that the solution lay in posting bond for him prior to his court hearing. Then I could walk out as if I were Wilbur.

I presented this scheme to Wilbur and he said he would go along with it for two thousand dollars. Since by this time Betsy had spent our loan money hiring a lawyer and paying bills, I asked my old friend Sonny to deliver the two thousand dollars to Wilbur's sister. After she verified receipt to Wilbur, he would then cooperate. Because the jail phones were often tapped, and because Sonny knew not to ask questions, neither he nor Betsy had any knowledge of our planned escape; it was just between Wilbur and me.

After several days Sonny raised the two thousand dollars but could not immediately deliver it. I then asked Betsy to pick up an envelope from Sonny and drop it off at the address he would give her. Wilbur's sister took the envelope from Betsy and notified Wilbur that she had the money. I then told Sonny to send a girl using an alias name to the bondsman and pay him $150 bond money for the release of Wilbur. I warned Sonny not to use his real name when he called the bondsman because Wilbur might skip town.

Saturday, four days after my arrest, the seldom-seen guard came back to the cell thirty minutes before midnight and called for Wilbur. Wilbur pretended to be asleep and I walked out in his place. The guard escorted me to the basement where I put on Wilbur's ill-fitting clothes. While there, I went before the magistrate and swore that I would be in court the following Monday. I was so nervous I misspelled Wilbur's last name when I signed it. Then the guard walked me to the door and released me. I have always been amazed that anyone would fail to suspect a man who misspelled his own name and wore a shirt three sizes too small that could hardly be buttoned, and pants six inches above the ankles.

I ran a block to the Holiday Inn and stopped a drunk staggering across the parking lot to his car. I told him I'd give him fifty dollars for a ride about ten miles away by expressway. The way he was driving, we were lucky we got there without being arrested or having a wreck. I gave him directions to a place within two blocks of my shop. When he stopped at the traffic light I jumped out and ran.

I picked up some petty cash stashed in my office and took my daughter's car which had just been repaired. It was very fortunate for me that the mechanic had returned it while I was in jail, and that my daughter had not yet picked it up. I even had some nice clothes and a company American Express card just waiting to be used. I was out of there driving Robin's car within minutes. I decided to worry later about getting the car back to her, since she didn't even know it had been repaired and returned.

I drove to Baltimore, Maryland. Early the next morning I left Robin's car in the long-term parking lot, got on a plane to Tampa, Florida, and caught a limo to St. Petersburg to meet an old friend willing to help me. After all those years of hard work I was back on the lam. Depressing as it was, however, my relief in being out of jail offered compensation. With little hope of obtaining justice within the Port City criminal justice system, I felt I had no other choice.

Within a week I obtained new ID, rented a cheap apartment, and began working for an electrical contractor, wiring houses and doing service changes in the St. Petersburg area. My boss, Dennis, was a fine man; I liked working for him and he appreciated my work. It was particularly nice that someone else had to worry about the book work, payroll, and accounts receivable, as I had done before.

I missed Betsy terribly and found myself drinking heavily to avoid thinking about her and wondering how all this would end. I knew the Port City criminal justice system and its people were bad, but they were yet to show me just how really bad they could be. But how could *I* call *anyone else* bad? It seemed I had been bad all my life. I was certainly in no position to condemn anyone else, much less discern who was the worst; bad is bad and wrong is wrong, whether committed by criminals, police, lawyers, or judges.

I had the shock of my life two weeks after my escape when I called Betsy and learned that she too had been arrested.

"Arrested?" I screamed into the phone. "For what?"

"For aiding your escape," she answered, as she began to cry. My mind was reeling. "I'm out on $40,000 bond. I was in jail only one night and my parents got me out."

In jail! I couldn't believe that sweet, innocent Betsy had been through the horrors of jail. I was enraged! I could also tell she was trying to be strong for me, yet was on the verge of breaking down. She said that the police had harassed her, following her around and threatening her. One policeman, a captain, no less, had told her he would ruin her life. It was inconceivable to me how anyone could do this to the most gentle, kind, compassionate person I had ever known.

Realizing how she had been victimized by my actions, I said, "My God, what have I done to cause such grief for this innocent girl?" But the agony was just beginning. I also learned the police had arrested Sonny for aiding my escape and set his bond at $15,000. They charged Wilbur as well, interrogating him with such ferocity that he broke down and told them everything he could, even implicating his own sister.

For his cooperation Wilbur was rewarded with three years in prison. If he had simply kept quiet or claimed to have been asleep, there was no way they could have convicted him or charged anyone else. Instead, he got himself and his sister in trouble, and his sister got Betsy in trouble with false information. I am sure Wilbur spent the next three years regretting his loose tongue. His false assumption was that the Port City police and prosecutors would do what they had solemnly promised.

As I reflected on Betsy's arrest and shared her pain, I seriously considered paying her ransom with my own surrender. This alternative was soon abandoned, however, by the realization that Port City was so bent on revenge that my surrender would not secure any leniency for Betsy; it would only provide them with one more trophy and whet their appetites.

I was scared for Betsy. I also was scared for myself when I heard that eighteen heavily armed FBI agents raided my parents' home at five o'clock in the morning. Although they knew that I never hurt anyone in my entire life and I never even carried a weapon, they put out a false report that I had vowed I would never be taken alive. I could see the handwriting on the wall and it was fearsome.

My fear was based on more than paranoid speculation. I remembered how agents had murdered an unarmed bank robber friend with no warning whatsoever. After killing him, they planted a gun in his hand. Unknown to them, two people in the house saw Jim walk out the front door and get gunned down. They witnessed the whole sorry spectacle, but, because they were afraid they would be next, they hid in the attic and kept quiet.

When my friends in St. Petersburg heard that Betsy, Wilbur, and Sonny had all been arrested for associating with me, they made it obvious that they wanted me to leave. They concluded that any authorities who wanted me badly enough to arrest Betsy would do the same to them. Virginia friends reported a changed attitude toward me. Police used to say, "Old Robert Witt is a slick nuisance, but we'll catch him sooner or later." Now it was, "We're going to get that S.O.B., dead or alive; if it's alive, he'll be sorry."

The question that echoed in my head over and over again was, "What in the world did Ox Skidmore tell them?" He had to tell them something fantastic to get the deal they gave him. Simply implicating me in a burglary wasn't enough to gain freedom from serious crimes such as assault with a deadly weapon while on parole.

Betsy too was getting paranoid. We became very cautious in our communications, numbering and labeling most of the pay phones we used. For instance, the pay phone at the Shell Station was "Shelly's house," and the one at the Virginia Steak House restaurant was "Ginny's house," etc… Mondays and Thursdays we went to pre-designated phones, and Betsy was always careful how she got there. We never used the same telephone twice in a row.

I consumed many rolls of quarters and we had numerous pay phone problems. We often missed each other, and the phones did not always function properly. We called it "the long distance bad phone blues," and we usually had back-up plans. More than once I spent my last ten dollars on a pay phone.

I began to feel increasingly unsafe in St. Petersburg. Sleep became more difficult, as my friends became more nervous. It was time to leave, but first I needed a car. Floyd, my landlord and a used car salesman, sold me a 1980 Mercury Zephyr for eight hundred dollars down and twenty–five dollars a week. It was perfect for me and took me all over the country. It was clean enough to keep me from looking like a bum, but not so flashy that I might appear to be a drug dealer. While travelling in other states with Florida tags, I definitely wanted to avoid being stopped as a suspected drug dealer.

After a month in St. Petersburg I packed my pots and pans and headed north, initially avoiding Virginia like the plague. I was always low on money and often picked up work as a convenience store cashier or laborer, load-ing and unloading long-distance trucks. These jobs pro-vided enough to keep me going but required long hours of very hard work. I traversed Tennessee, Kentucky, Indiana, then east through Pennsylvania and Maryland, with thoughts of Betsy drawing me like a magnet back to Virginia. I missed her terribly.

I stayed in Maryland for months, sneaking into Virginia several times to see her. This caused us both great anxiety, yet we simply could not stay away from each other. Realizing that I was pressing my luck, I headed back to Jacksonville, Florida. Because I did not feel comfortable there, I moved farther south to Bonita Springs, just south of Ft. Myers. Situated on the Gulf coast, its beauty was surpassed only by the hospitality of its fine people.

Because there was very little crime in that part of Florida, people didn't view strangers with suspicion. And best of all, it was a short distance to Miami, where Betsy periodically visited her stepfather in his Coconut Grove penthouse apartment. Several times when Betsy was visiting him, I parked my car and walked down the sidewalk looking up at the balcony, hoping to catch a glimpse of her. Knowing I often did this, she would amble out on the balcony and spot me. The meeting of our eyes produced moments of sheer magic.

Her Dad often sent Betsy out on a shopping spree and we would meet for majestic moments, strolling together through Coconut Grove arm in arm, stopping at cafes and trying to pretend that everything was all right. Once when she, her Dad, and a friend went to the movies to see *Biloxi Blues*, I also went and sat several rows behind Betsy so that we could make eye contact and meet at the concession stand for a quick kiss and hug. We were crazy in love.

I worked for several different people. One employer I particularly appreciated was a real estate investor named Dennis, different from the Dennis in St. Petersburg. Dennis bought old houses, fixed them up and sold them at a good profit. Because most of them were bank foreclosures and had been vacant for a long time, they were in serious need of repair. He also had many rental units needing maintenance. This kept me busy with all types of repairs.

I enjoyed this work and enjoyed Dennis' company. He and his girlfriend were great people and a lot of fun to be with. We often went out together for meals and a few beers. With them I could relax in spite of my circumstances. I wondered what they would have thought of me if they had known I was a fugitive.

Betsy and I kept waiting for her case to be dropped. In an effort to help her, I had her give the police a telephone number I had previously used in Indiana, in a place I knew was known to them but was then vacated. The commonwealth attorney in Port City had agreed to drop all charges against Betsy if the phone number put a lead on me, which it did.

When the prosecutor recommended charges be dropped, however, the judge refused. He violated his prior promise because the sheriff was so angry about my escape that he had gone to the judge, reporting a rumored payoff. The sheriff warned that leniency toward Betsy would give credence to the rumor. The judge then refused to drop the charge.

Soon thereafter the sheriff petitioned the television show, *America's Most Wanted*, to air a segment on me. Headlines in the newspaper of September 20, 1988, read, *"Port City Sheriff Turns to TV Show to Find Escapee."* Faye Johnson, the staff reporter, wrote, "The convicted burglar who escaped from the city jail one year ago Monday, leaving the sheriff's staff red in the face..."

In the afternoon edition she changed "red in the face" to, "embarrassed," possibly due to the sheriff's objections. According to Faye Johnson, he constantly objected to any negative reference to himself. Athough I didn't see any difference between "red faced" and "embarrassed," he was angry because colleagues and friends as far away as California had called, teasing him for running a jail where prisoners could simply walk out. I called a family friend who told me about the article. I couldn't believe they would put me on *America's Most Wanted*, since that program seemed to feature violent people who had committed vicious crimes; I never did any violence to anyone in my life, and certainly did not merit exposure on nationwide TV. I decided it was time to leave Southwest Florida, since many people knew me well enough to identify me from television. In preparation for my next flight, I traded my old Mercury for a new Dodge truck. I selected one with a camper top for sleeping and arranged monthly payments of $295 per month. I packed my essential possessions in the truck, put the remainder in storage, and headed for a place I had never even heard of: Gulf Shores, Alabama.

During this time of transition, Betsy and I received another big shock. She had always dreamed of having a baby but had accepted the medical opinion that previous difficulties in youth prevented her conception. Now, of all times, we were to have a baby! When the drug store pregnancy test gave a positive report we could hardly believe it. In fact, I doubted the test results; tests could be wrong. But this one was true.

Although I had dreamed of marrying Betsy and having children, and although we talked about it almost as soon as we met, now seemed to be the worst time to bring a new life into the world. Yet, in spite of our dire circumstances, we were elated—more than a little scared, but elated, nonetheless.

Now, more than ever, I didn't want Betsy away from me. Because I always saw Betsy as being so delicate, like a beautiful flower, I would never want her in this cruel world alone, especially at a time when she would be needing lots of love and protective care.

When, in the very beginning of her pregnancy, Betsy fell victim to morning sickness, I was distressed. Being pregnant is one of the scariest things I've ever had to face. I say that in the first person because I felt I was going through everything with her, as if I too were pregnant.

When I left Naples that last week of August, 1988, Betsy was back in Virginia staying with her sister. I felt incomplete and depressed without her. I earnestly hoped that Port City would drop charges against her, thus freeing her to join me. Their harassment of her seemed irrational, excessive, and unjustified. And after her family had paid fifteen thousand dollars up front, her lawyer showed little incentive in pursuing her case. It appeared from my subjective point of view that the entire Port City judicial system acted vindictively.

Harassment came in many ways, like the day the SWAT team came to the house where Betsy and her sister were staying. Some twenty strong, they took Betsy and her sister out in the street and made them stand for hours while all the team tore the house inside-out, pretending they were looking for me. With no legitimate reason to believe I was there, it seemed designed to break Betsy's will.

The actions of Port City authorities seemed especially jaded when compared with Betsy's impeccable character. She has always been a kind, truthful, loving person. She has such an altruistic commitment to helping other people that she would prefer being hurt herself rather contribute to the hurt of anyone else. I remember how she pressed me to pick up hitchhikers because she was afraid no one else would do so; she would give her last few dollars to a beggar, or scold me whenever I was critical of anyone else, even those who persecuted her so relentlessly.

I tried not to dwell on these things as I drove up I-75 toward the Florida Panhandle. Since preoccupation with our troubles could leave me too frustrated to function effectively, I had to control my thought patterns more carefully than ever. With a child on the way, I could not afford to be careless and make mistakes that might jeopardize my family. And the thought of a baby was awesome.

At that time I could hardly imagine how to fulfill my parental responsibilities while fleeing society. I tried to picture Betsy pregnant, or me holding a baby, or Betsy and me tending a son or daughter. I would pronounce the word "Baby" as if I'd just learned how to say it. I felt rather foolish as a forty-year-old fugitive about to have a baby. At least once I remember exclaiming, "Oh my God!" And I was not taking His Name in vain.

I drove across the Florida Panhandle to Pensacola with baby thoughts dancing in my head. Eventually, reality returned me to the mission at hand: finding a safe place to live. I drove to Pensacola Beach, found several nice campgrounds, and spent the night in one. Having just bought a nice tent for ten dollars at a flea market in St. Petersburg, I enjoyed camping inexpensively. Months later, when forced to take refuge in it for survival in the bitter cold, it was not so enjoyable.

The next morning I headed for Alabama. From Pensacola anyone could then drive twenty-five miles on the beach, just like a road, all the way into Gulf Shores, Alabama. I never realized that about forty miles of Alabama is on the Gulf Coast, all the way to the bay into

Mobile. I thoroughly enjoyed browsing through the area and was fortunate to rent a nice beach condo for the off-season rate of $295 per month. Completely furnished, this seemed an excellent place for Betsy during her pregnancy. The following morning a strange thing happened. As bizarre as it sounds, I awakened with morning sickness, a phenomenon that was repeated several times. I had once heard of such a strange thing but doubted it was possible until I personally experienced it.

After paying a deposit on the condo, I headed back to South Florida to complete job commitments, collect my pay, and move everything to Gulf Shores. Betsy planned to drive down and stay for a week or two this time.

Arriving back in Naples late Wednesday afternoon, I called Betsy at our 4:30 appointed time. She told me she was just leaving and asked me to meet her halfway. Although already fatigued from my travel, I headed six hundred miles north to our familiar prearranged I-95 rendezvous in Georgia. I arrived at 3:00 a.m., half an hour ahead of Betsy. It was always wonderful to see her again, yet every rendezvous began with great anxiety until we knew we had not been spotted.

As I saw her red truck angle off the I-95 exit, I stayed in place till I knew she had not been followed. When we felt all was safe, we pulled our vehicles to the edge of the gas station parking lot and ran into each other's arms. We hugged, kissed, stretched a bit, drank a soda from the all-night convenience store, gassed up, and planned our next moves.

Since I had the comfortable truck, we exchanged vehicles and followed each other down I-95 toward Tampa, alert for any signals we might send each other. After traveling for two days with no sleep, it was all I could do to stay awake. We drove straight through to

Tampa, arriving totally exhausted about noon on Thursday, the first of September 1988.

In Tampa we called our friend, Pam, and went to her new house just as she and her boyfriend, Doug, began moving in. After the briefest of greetings, Betsy and I found a corner of the floor free of packing boxes and "crashed" for some much needed sleep. Several hours later, about 1:00 a.m., I kissed my sleeping beauty goodbye and headed back to Naples to finalize business there. Only then could I return for Betsy and usher her into our lovely new beach condo in Gulf Shores, Alabama. I was excited about sharing such a beautiful place with her, and longed for the stability it could provide.

I met Dennis in Fort Myers, just north of Naples, where we finished renovating some houses he had bought on Seminole Drive. From there I went to Naples, finished a job there, collected my pay, and cashed a check. That afternoon I rented a tow bar from a rental shop on Mercantile Road to tow Betsy's truck from Tampa to Alabama, thus enabling us to ride together. By the grace of God, people involved in these events of Friday, September 2, 1988, later verified my presence with them and thus saved me from spending the remainder of my life in a South Carolina prison for false accusation of armed robbery, eight hundred miles away.

Back in Tampa on Friday night, I connected Betsy's truck to mine in the pouring rain and we left for Gulf Shores the next day. We arrived just in time to pick up the key before the rental office closed. The rental office was run by two gracious ladies, Louise and Patricia, who did everything possible to make us welcome and comfortable in their condo.

My expectations were fulfilled when Betsy expressed delight with our beach home; it was just perfect. Constructed on pilings in an isolated area, it provided space to park our trucks underneath and enjoy safety, comfort, and peace, at least for a short interlude. The first floor had a kitchen, dining area and bedroom, while the second floor had a den and master bedroom adjacent to a sun deck overlooking the Gulf of Mexico.

A week later, on September 9, Betsy and I were married at the Candle Light Chapel in Pensacola. I was very nervous and Betsy cried. Although we would have preferred a church ceremony with friends and family in Virginia, it was still a nice service we will always cherish.

During that period Betsy was sick every morning and sometimes several times a day. I felt great empathy for her and much frustration that I could not alleviate her discomfort.

News from Virginia indicated intense curiosity about Betsy's whereabouts. With great reluctance we therefore decided she had to return, at least for a while. It pained me beyond words to let her go, and we were both apprehensive about the future. Being pregnant made her more emotional than she normally was, and this, in turn, increased my anxiety. The uncertainty of it all was taking its toll on both of us.

The separations of this period were terrible. In addition to the absence we deplored, Betsy was burdened by dishonest pretense. For her own survival, she had to convince family, friends, and authorities that she hated me and never wanted to see me again. I was particularly upset that her sister, with whom she was living, kept pressing her to date various men her sister kept lining up. There was no way she could pre-empt such unwanted advances with the simple boundary definition: "I am married."

I got a job as a waiter making money on tips while also doing electrical repair work as it came available. I saved every penny I could get my hands on, anticipating doctor's bills and hospital expenses for Betsy's delivery. She planned to slip away for another two-week visit in October. Port City court officials were still delaying her case and, for some unknown reason, her lawyer had agreed to a continuance. With such inadequate evidence against Betsy, the commonwealth attorney perpetuated her anxiety through delaying tactics. I could never understand why her defense attorney put up with such an obvious ploy.

Our next rendezvous was to be in Charlotte, North Carolina, October 7, 1988, at the Red Roof Inn on Billy Graham Parkway, as close to 2:00 p.m. as we could both make it. I was going to hitchhike so we could drive back together.

The pressure of everything was really frustrating for both Betsy and me at this point. Our frustration occasionally found expression in arguments that even included accusations of past suspicions of unfaithfulness. Reason always overcame the irrationality of our frustration, leading to apologies and reaffirmation of loving trust. When depressed, we were able to encourage each other with recognition that Betsy's pregnancy was emotionally taxing for both of us.

While hitchhiking to North Carolina, I became acutely aware of a new fear caused by a slowly moving police car and two officers staring at me. Terror gripped me with such force I almost broke and ran into the woods. Just before the police could stop to question me or I could run, another car stopped and picked me up. What a close call! In addition to my loss of sleep before leaving, I had smoked some unusually strong marijuana offered by someone on the beach. It left me depressed, jumpy and paranoid; I was stoned.

In anticipation of a possible shakedown by the police, I repeatedly reviewed in my mind the fictitious details of the alias personality I had concocted. I had neglected to find out if it was legal to hitchhike in Alabama. I wondered if my picture was plastered on the walls of all the state police headquarters across the eastern states.

After several short rides, I found myself stranded at a truck stop somewhere south of Montgomery. Too scared to stay in the truck stop across the highway, I stood on the ramp of the interstate, thumbing for a ride. For more than five hours car after car and truck after truck passed me by. As the weary hours dragged on, paranoia and depression mingled together. I feared I was going to lose Betsy and I would soon be caught, maybe killed by the police or FBI. I imagined myself in a coffin, with my family in the front rows of the church, listening to the priest's attempt to comfort them by saying that I would never again have to run from the law or anything else.

Meanwhile, another man was approaching my spot on the lonely interstate highway, a man who was destined to change my life and the life of my wife for all time. Like me, he was lonely and depressed, at least at that moment. Unlike me, he was a Christian who knew that the power of God can dispel our depression and replace all our negativism with His love and joy as we are obedient to the leading of the Spirit. Seven years later he described his encounter with Harold Capps (the alias I was using at that time) in the following words:

Normally, I never pick up riders. In the last fifteen years I can account for only one person I ever picked up on the highway and that was Harold Capps. I was northbound on I-65 approaching Georgina, Alabama, when I got the feeling that I should get off at the next exit. Call it a voice from within, or my Protector, or perhaps the Lord's voice in the wind, it was very real to me. I've learned to obey such feelings, so I promptly got off. When I went up the ramp I had no idea what I was supposed to do, nor did I know where I was supposed to go once I left the highway.

After I left the highway the feeling left me, so I turned left, crossing over the Interstate. I stopped at a little run-down gas station and bought a Coke I really didn't want. The place was dirty, damp, and had large roaches crawling all over. I went back to my truck and headed for the highway. On the side of the entrance ramp was a man with his thumb up, asking for a ride. The feeling that I should pick him up returned even stronger than before.

I didn't like that idea at all, and I struggled against it. I wasn't in the mood to talk to anyone at all; I just didn't want company. I also knew it wasn't a safe thing to do, not because he looked mean or dangerous, but because he was a stranger. I had always been told by Mom and Dad not to pick up hitchhikers, but I stopped anyway and let him in. I'm sure he felt my uneasiness; I just wanted to be alone that night.

We drove seventy miles through Montgomery, Alabama, toward Atlanta. I don't remember talking very much during the first part of the trip, just little bits and pieces about where he was going, and chitchat like that.

As we left Montgomery, I said that I didn't usually pick up riders, that he should thank God that I did it this time. Looking back, our conversation seemed to gradually become Christian witnessing, but at the time

I wasn't aware of it. One comment led to another regarding God; I spoke from my heart, even at the risk of offending this stranger.

The farther we traveled, the more involved we became. He asked one question after another, each getting more and more in depth about Christ and salvation. With every question I answered about Christ, about salvation, about prayer and the Holy Spirit, my feelings got more intense. I felt the biggest rush of "Good" I'd ever experienced. I'm still not sure how I drove the truck because my thoughts became so involved in Christ that I only remember driving small stretches at a time.

Before we got to Atlanta, Harold asked me to help him ask God for forgiveness and to pray with him. My heart swelled as I heard Harold ask Christ to come into his life to save him. On a dark and timeless night, right in the cab of my diesel truck, we prayed together and received the blessing of a lifetime. Joyfully, I watched God move a man from the darkness of night into the light of everlasting life.

From that very moment I could see a real difference in Harold. He had a new inner peace anyone could see. I'd seen many people receive Christ before, but never one like this; he seemed really changed, really different from the man I'd first let into my truck.

I reassured Harold that Christ's promise and His gift of everlasting life were real. It was a gift that could never be taken away by any man or any spirit, and we rejoiced together, talking as if we'd known each other all our lives.

Then I got another surprise I hadn't expected. Harold asked me if he could tell his wife about Christ and all he'd learned that night. Of course, I was over-

joyed. He wanted to know if he could show her the plan of salvation, or if someone who knew a lot about the Bible should do it. I explained that he should follow the Holy Spirit within, that he should tell her as I had told him, but only if she wanted to hear it. I explained that if he followed his feelings the Holy Spirit would do the rest. He was so excited and happy that he seemed to have a visible glow about him. I'd never seen such an eagerness to learn about Christ. I was truly thankful that God had used me to plant the seed of His redemption.

Afterward, Harold did write me, telling his story over ten pages or so. He described all his troubles and the risk he was taking. He talked like a new person, a person who wanted to live for Christ. He talked about wanting to face up to everything and get right with God. The day I received his letter was a second blessing for me. He told me how he'd led his wife to Christ as soon as he had met up with her. He said they cried together and wept with joyful hearts over their newly found life." (Reported by Dan "Ricochet" Barnhill, Rex, Georgia, September 21, 1994).

During the past seven years I have remembered that momentous midnight encounter with Ricochet, and the subsequent encounter with Christ. I remember his questions about my inner peace and my life direction, both of which I longed for but did not have. I remember his explanation of Christ's crucifixion as the ultimate expression of how much God loves me. I remember how I recognized for the first time in my life the root cause of my futility and misery. My heart burned within me as I was overcome with fear and conviction. I remember feeling that if I did not obtain relief I might jump out of the truck as it sped down the Interstate.

Then he got scary. He told me that God had told him to pick me up. He also said that Satan wanted to control my life and the lives of my loved ones. He even said the devil wanted to destroy my wife and me. If, however, I committed my life to Christ, Satan could not then touch us. The thought of some demonic power trying to hurt Betsy was mind-boggling, yet the persecution and legal chaos then swirling around her and her family could not be explained in rational human terms alone.

I remember feeling that Ricochet knew all about me and my fears and depression. He had expounded on Romans 10:9, *"If you confess with your mouth the Lord Jesus and believe in your heart that God raised Him from the dead, you will be saved."* I remember how I could hardly wait for him to finish those words so that I could confess Jesus and express my belief that God had raised Him from the dead.

During previous days in prison I once joined in Bible study with some Christians, but it never changed my attitude nor had any lasting impact on my behavior; no real commitment was ever made. But now I knew something unique had happened. Call it redemption or salvation, or whatever, I knew that I had communed with God, my Creator, and I felt forgiven. I felt an awesome love from God and for God. I suddenly felt safe and believed that somehow no harm could overcome Betsy or me. I could hardly wait to see Betsy and share this "salvation" with her; nothing else seemed important. I prayed we would both make it safely to our meeting place.

After praying with me, Ricochet let me out in Atlanta, Georgia, at one of the biggest truck stops in the country. Once again the truck stop atmosphere worried me, with all the police coming and going. I walked down to the Interstate entrance ramp and stood another four hours waiting for my next ride. Although God had surely touched my soul, He seemed in no hurry to transport my body with another ride. Perhaps He was simply providing time for me to reflect on the wonder of what had just happened.

It took several rides and many hours to travel the ten miles through Atlanta. Finally, another trucker picked me up at the rest stop and took me all the way to Charlotte, right to the front of the Red Roof Inn where I was to meet Betsy. Perhaps God had been testing my newly found faith, I thought. I began to realize that God has a purpose in everything, even when we are too blind to see it and too self-centered to want to see it.

I checked in and told the desk clerk I was expecting my wife. Within a couple of hours Betsy was there and I immediately sensed that she was in the same frame of mind I had been in *before* my encounter with the Lord: tense, depressed, and forlorn.

I terribly feared losing Betsy. Yet, on the other hand, I had often wished I had the courage to let her go for her own good. My chaotic situation was fast engulfing her; I told myself that if I really loved her I would put her welfare first and terminate our relationship.

As I saw Betsy in the doorway of the motel I speculated that my encounter with the Lord might end the struggles of our hectic relationship. In light of my conversion, she might conclude that I had lost my sanity; she might then cut loose on her own. Thus I decided I should get right to the heart of the matter.

"Before you say anything," I said while holding up my hands, "I need to tell you what has happened to me." She sat on the side of the bed as I related to her, as best I could remember, all that Ricochet had related to me.

When I finished, we were both down on our knees weeping and praying. On that same day Betsy also accepted the Lord Jesus Christ as her Savior.

At this point we both naively believed that God would instantly transform the awful mess we had made of our lives, replacing it with harmony and good will. As we sought to follow Christ and learn obedience to God's Word, however, we also learned that Christ as our *SAVIOR* is not enough; He must be *LORD* of all. Surrendering control of our lives to allow His divine rule proved more difficult than we could imagine. During the ensuing pilgrimage we were still to face our most painful trials and tribulations. Yet our God, in His most gentle way, also made us face ourselves in the process of spiritual growth and maturity.

CHAPTER 6

RUNNING AND PREGNANT

FROM TWO TO THREE

Fortunately, Betsy's pregnancy did not prevent her from driving or riding over the lengthy highways we had to travel. Unfortunately, it repeatedly produced nausea and illness in inappropriate places such as restaurants and crowded parking lots. Such nauseous episodes caused embarrassment and loss of appetite to all. During Betsy's first trimester we both lost weight. I was frustrated by my inability to cure her sickness, but grateful that I could at least stand beside her during her difficulty.

Back at Gulf Shores we tried to relax and cultivate our inner growth through joint Bible reading. I went to a Christian book store and bought numerous books and Bibles to learn what had happened to us, and what we should expect and do in the future. Although spiritually immature, we were very serious about living our new lifestyle with Christ.

I got a job with an electrical contractor in Mobile, wiring a new shopping center in Gulf Shores. This job was so close to our living quarters that Betsy often brought me lunch. I learned from a fellow worker about better-paying jobs in Demopolis, Alabama, with one of the largest electrical contractors in the country, head-quartered in Baton Rouge, Louisiana. Enlarging a paper mill just outside of Demopolis, they hired me for more money ($12.50 an hour). They held out the possibility of staying with the company, moving around the country on other jobs.

Betsy and I packed up together this time, driving both trucks to Demopolis, a small pulp mill town, jokingly referred to as "the metropolis of Demopolis." Although I had a pay check due from the Gulf Shores job, a large check coming from Naples, and another from Pensacola, I had nothing at the time but pocket change. I therefore called a friend and had him wire five hundred dollars by Western Union. I drove all the way back to Pensacola to pick it up since I didn't want anyone, not even the friend I trusted, to know exactly where we were.

Unable to find an apartment we could afford, Betsy and I met a woman who owned some land on a river where she let us camp. For two weeks we slept in a tent and cooked on a gas stove. She let us bathe and sometimes eat at her house. Both she and her son, Eddie, were very good to us, assisting us in every way possible. One day Eddie gave us a little puppy that seemed to have been abused and half scared to death. We named her "Hattie," and she joined our little family of fugitives. Betsy was finally able to help Hattie overcome her fear, and she became like our child.

Then the bad news came. After continued pressure and input from the Port City Sheriff, "America's Most Wanted" was ready to feature me on their Sunday night show. Although I knew how zealously he was pressing the hunt for me and pursuing the case against my wife, I hoped his efforts for television coverage would be unproductive.

When the newspapers back in Virginia announced that I would be featured on television in a week, we knew we had to immediately flee once again. I fabricated a story about a death in the family, collected my pay, and we went back to Pensacola to collect the other money from my last job there. After living out of a tent in chilly weather, not eating properly and not sleeping well, we were weary, anxious, and irrational. Now we feared the television exposure and its possible consequences.

We made our way to Georgia, not sure where we were going, and stopped at a motel about thirty miles outside of Atlanta. I wore sun glasses and a hat to camouflage my appearance to others. We were pleased to get a room at the far end of the motel, adjacent to a field where we could let Hattie relieve herself, away from auto traffic and away from other people.

We went to a grocery store and bought sandwich food and cereal, and dog food for Hattie. We rented a storage bin large enough for Betsy's truck and most of our belongings. We then hibernated in our room all day Sunday, trying to suppress our anxiety while waiting for the dreaded television program. Finally, at seven o'clock, it came on. Our hearts were pounding as we heard the commentator intone, "Tonight, you [the viewers] can help us catch Robert C. Witt ..." There I was, side and front profiles of my face covering the TV screen. It didn't say much, only that I was wanted for pulling a $200,000 heist and escaping from jail, but I pictured in my mind's eye all the people we had known in Florida and Gulf Shores reaching for their telephones and exclaiming, "Hey, that's Harold Capps" (my alias name).

I tried not to let Betsy know how scared I was. I continued thinking about our unborn child and wondering if all the stress could hurt it. As I attempted to reassure Betsy that everything would be okay, we were suddenly distracted by Hattie getting sick. She lost her dinner and lay deathly still. This, in addition to the television expose` and her pregnancy, was too much for Betsy. She was so upset I agreed to let her take Hattie to a veterinarian. We looked in the Yellow Pages and found one still open, and Betsy took Hattie to the animal hospital while I stayed at the motel with knots in my stomach. I shaved off my beard and gave myself a crew cut. It was the first time in over a dozen years I had been without a beard.

The next morning Hattie was well and we had calmed down, even though the night was sleepless. I had repeatedly jumped up and run to the window every time I heard a car pull up during the night. I loaded the truck and carried Betsy to a friend's house in Virginia, leaving her there and hoping she could convince everyone she had never been gone. After she left I felt lonely, despondent, and scared. I desperately needed money to continue our flight to parts unknown until the heat died down from my television debut.

As Hattie and I headed back to Florida, I determined to get rid of the truck and change ID to another name once again. It was a gamble driving around in an identified truck and using a nationally known alias, but I had no choice. I was beginning to feel very desperate. On the return trip south, my sense of desperation was increasing as I tried to decide what I should do next. I became so obsessed with police cars that my heart pounded every time one passed me on the interstate.

Arriving in Atlanta, I rented an efficiency apartment for a week. It took several days before Hattie would get near the truck; we were both sick of living in a vehicle. Then the nightmare intensified. When I called Betsy at her girlfriend's house, she reported that the police were looking for her to arrest her. As a result of television exposure, the people who married us in Florida and others in Alabama had reported that Betsy was with me. Now they had revoked Betsy's bond and wanted to put her in jail. She was fearful and distraught. I told her to book passage on the next available flight to Charlotte, North Carolina, under a pseudonym and check into a certain motel under yet a different alias. I placed Hattie in a dog kennel and left my truck in storage, retrieved Betsy's truck from storage, and drove to Charlotte. This was done because her truck was less likely to be identified.

After meeting at the designated motel, we began a soul-searching analysis of the entire situation, examining all of our possible courses of action and assessing the consequences. Unfortunately, there were only two choices: Betsy had to either go to jail or she could go on the run with me. If she went to jail she would undoubtedly be detained till after her pregnancy and then have her baby taken from her. The thought of pregnancy in jail was bad enough, but the prospect of losing our precious child, yet unborn, was entirely too painful to contemplate.

The fact that Betsy and I were now Christians, desiring to know and follow the will of God, made the decision all the more difficult. Scripture clearly teaches compliance with civil authority: *"Let everyone be in subjection to the authorities....He who resists the authorities resists what God has appointed"* (Romans 12:1-2). And since I had not masterminded the heist as the police claimed, why not go to court and plead my case? Furthermore, if we were truly committed to God, why would we not be willing to trust Him with the verdict of the court?

The struggle was intense! In the end, our newly found faith was insufficient to overcome our distrust of the Port City authorities. Their many broken promises led us to conclude that a fair trial was impossible. If it had involved me alone, I could have endured anything they would inflict on me, but now there were three of us. So, with great anxiety and trust in God, we headed west, all the way to New Mexico.

CHAPTER 7

FUGITIVES IN A DISTANT LAND

NEW MEXICO

With newly found feelings of security, Betsy and I wanted to know all about New Mexico, especially the area around Albuquerque. In the mountains of Tijeras, about twenty-five miles southeast of town, we discovered an area we immediately loved, beautiful beyond anything we had ever seen. We began looking for affordable land and found a one-acre wooded lot for less than two thousand dollars. I planned to buy the lot, build a house, sell it, and with that money do it all over somewhere else, again and again.

Having worked around construction all my non-incarcerated life, I had done every aspect of it at one time or another. What better way to earn a living and avoid capture? I would be working for myself, away from the scrutiny of police or other authorities.

Although our limited funds would not cover the total project, I knew that we could borrow the money needed for completion once the house was framed, the well dug, and septic tank installed. Many people lend money against collateral, without credit rating or character investigation of the owner. All one has to do is get the classified section of any large city newspaper and find the heading of "*Money to Lend.*" The interest is high, but that is the price for people in our condition. Betsy had confidence in my ability to work and manage, so we agreed that this was our best hope.

Upon purchase of the lot, we discovered why it was so cheap. There was no electricity available, and water at seventy–five hundred feet above sea level was scarce and expensive. We were quoted prices of five thousand dollars for a well and seven thousand dollars for electricity. By copying my original Real Masters Electricians Card on a copy machine at the local library, then whiting out my true name and replacing it with "Wayne Crews," and by making a copy of that copy, I was then able to get a permit from the power company to do the work myself. The county also required a test, which I passed quite easily.

With a lot of ingenuity and shopping around for materials, I was able to get power to our building site for fifteen hundred dollars. By hiring well diggers during their slack season, we were able to drill a three-hundred foot well and install a submersible pump for less than thirty-five hundred dollars.

We were also fortunate in meeting a neighbor who became a great friend and supporter, lending me tools and letting me tap into his electricity. He was appropriately called "Junk Yard Bob" because of the diverse building materials strewn throughout his two acres of the mountain. Bob and his dog, Mutt, the biggest black Lab I've ever seen, lived alone and liked it that way. Bob had a big heart and would do anything for his friends, yet never wanted anything in return.

By Christmas, Betsy, five months pregnant, and I had employed shovels, axes, picks, and chain saw to clear a driveway and building site. We then hired a man with a little Bobcat to grade the building site, paying thirty dollars an hour for three hours. We put up batter boards and leveled and squared our footing trenches with a string level and a measuring tape. Although this old-fashioned method took two days, it was square, level, and cheap: four dollars for string, level, and measuring tape; fifty dollars for the chain saw and other tools. My previous experience in dealing with pawn brokers proved helpful, since we bought 90% of our tools from pawn shops.

Additional assistance resulted from picking up a hitchhiker named Frank. Frank was a leftover hippie from the 1960s era. He was likeable, knowledgeable about construction, and a good worker as long as we could keep him sober. He helped frame the house for five dollars an hour. He also introduced us to one of his neighbors, an experienced midwife. It was truly amazing how God brought all these diverse people into our lives at just the right time to meet our needs in such a marvelous way.

Before the well was dug, we imported water in gallon milk jugs to mix mortar for the foundation. We worked cement only a few hours each day, due to the early morning and late evening freeze. Our neighbors in town looked at us askance as we lugged dozens of milk jugs in the back of the station wagon every morning. We mixed mortar the old fashioned way, in a wheelbarrow. Cement and building materials were hauled up the mountain in the station wagon.

At this time I returned to Atlanta to retrieve my truck from storage, since the storage rent would soon be due. I later wished I had carried it to the closest parking lot and left it there, an idea I originally had but regrettably abandoned. I left Betsy in the company of Hattie and was promised by neighbors that they would help her. I flew to Atlanta, retrieved the truck, and emptied our storage bin.

Several weeks earlier I had gone to a urologist because I was having urinary trouble. After x-rays and an assortment of other tests, he attempted a cystoscope. Through clumsiness, this doctor severed an obstruction that was later diagnosed as a stricture. From the time I left his office I was in great pain and bled profusely. I could not see him for another week, during which time infection spread to my prostate. By then, I was much worse than when he initially treated me. When I told him of my impending trip, he gave me some medicine and said, "Take it easy."

The morning I left to return to New Mexico I was desperately ill. The farther I went the sicker I became. Sitting in the truck became increasingly painful; the inflamed prostate left me feeling like a hot poker had penetrated my rectum. At the outskirts of Clinton, Oklahoma, I knelt on the side of the road and threw up. I went into Clinton and found a Dr. Hausendorf, who immediately recognized the problem and prescribed medication of Ciprofloxacin for the infection. He also prescribed medication for the sickness and ordered me to bed. I rented a room in the nearest motel, called Betsy, and went to sleep, only to wake up in the middle of the night nauseous and throwing up.

I wanted badly to be home with Betsy; I knew she would nurse me back to health and make me comfortable. So, in spite of the doctor's orders to stay in bed, I got up and headed for Albuquerque. It was the longest drive I've ever made. I was extremely sick the whole way, and very relieved to get back home.

Betsy has always believed in the value of health foods, naturally and organically grown, and herbal medicines. Having worked in health food restaurants and stores and having studied natural healing, she had acquired basic knowledge of the art. Even before I returned home she had stocked up on medicines and foods she used to treat me. Thus she had me well again within a week.

Soon after I returned to Albuquerque, we found a little cabin for rent up in the mountains, less than half a mile by road and a quarter mile through the woods from our building site. The owners, Debbie and Ray, charged us only $125 a month. They became close friends, some of the most wonderful people we've ever known. Debbie and Ray had recently built their own house and had an infant son. Thus, the four of us shared common interests and experiences, as new home builders and as new and expectant parents.

Our cabin had one room with a small kitchenette and a loft the size of a king-size bed. The loft was intended for a bed, but we used it for storage, since I was afraid to let Betsy climb up and down the rickety ladder. It had a small bathroom with a shower. Because the only source of heat was a big stone fireplace, I always kept it supplied with chopped wood. Our bed almost covered the whole room. A chair in a corner left just enough space to squeeze around it. We loved that cozy little cabin. Except on rare warm nights, we went to bed with a roaring fire in the fireplace. Hattie slept by the front door, away from the heat, maintaining dutiful vigilance at her guard post.

Being isolated in late pregnancy and often in snowy weather, we sought an affordable four-wheel drive vehicle. We found a 1962 International Scout pickup for six hundred dollars. It was in bad shape but it did get us up and down the mountain in snow and ice. As money began to dwindle, Betsy and I learned to stretch every dollar to its limit. Living closer to the house under construction saved us five dollars a day on gas alone. Our rent was less than half what it had been in the city, we had no heating bill, and electricity was only twenty-five dollars a month.

We scheduled trips to town less frequently, buying groceries, supplies, and building materials all at once. We joined Price Club so we could buy at reduced prices, and a health food co-op where natural foods were nearly as cheap as regular foods. We ate a lot of beans, brown rice, oatmeal, and leftovers. Because Betsy is a fabulous cook, our meals were still appetizing and enjoyable.

Although we were healthy, happy, and free, we were always apprehensive. As Sundays drew near and time for the dreaded program, *America's Most Wanted*, we became increasingly anxious. Television reception was so poor it could hardly be seen without use of a satellite dish. Nevertheless, we usually called friends in Florida or Virginia for advanced warning in case we had been featured on the earlier East Coast telecasts. If so, they could warn us to flee before we would be seen on New Mexico television.

One Sunday, after a particularly hard day, we neglected to call back East for our usual alert and were petrified to see the fuzzy, static-ridden pictures of ourselves on TV. I tried to calm Betsy and avoid showing the fear that gripped me.

To further our shock, the commentator, John Walsh, said the police identified me as the culprit who robbed a credit union in South Carolina in September 1988. "So now," Mr. Walsh was saying with dramatic flair, "Witt is also wanted for armed robbery." In reality, I had never been in South Carolina except to drive through it on the interstate highway. Further, I had never used a gun to rob anybody of anything in my entire life.

With near panic we threw clothing and food into bags and suitcases as fast as we could. We locked the cabin and drove down a path near Bob's house, hiding the pickup in thick brush where it could not be seen. I hid the Dodge truck in dense woods behind the new house. Thank God, it wasn't snowing. I walked Betsy through the woods to Bob's house, feigning a visit while she and Bob watched a movie. I made trips back and forth through the woods to the cabin to see if the police had come. Since few people knew we knew Bob, we felt a little safer there for the time being.

That night we tried sleeping in the car. Between fitful cat naps, I was running back and forth with Hattie through the woods to watch the house. The next night we set up the tent and the gas stove. I sneaked back to the cabin to get more blankets, hoping and praying Betsy wouldn't catch cold. She was very courageous, crying occasionally, but never for long.

We began to pray and read the Psalms together, especially those which described David's plea to God for protection while fleeing from King Saul. Betsy's faith and trust in God was much stronger than mine, and she refused to even consider that God would allow us to be captured before the baby was born and in good hands.

I hardly slept at all, watching Hattie closely for any warning of movement outside the tent. At the slightest noise, Hattie's ears perked up and I would slide out of the tent and creep around the perimeter to insure that all was well. At least four times during the night I would bundle up and hike through the woods to the cabin, checking closely for a police stakeout. Hattie seemed to know exactly what we were doing as she scouted around, never getting more than twenty feet ahead of me.

I would whisper "Good dog" to Hattie as we circled the cabin and watched every shadow. No human could have been in those woods surrounding the cabin without Hattie knowing about it. I believe she could smell a human a quarter mile away. In addition to our ground surveillance, I also listened to the police scanner.

As Hattie and I returned to the tent after each reconnaissance, I was careful to make a certain warning noise to avoid scaring Betsy, bundled up in half a dozen blankets.

At seventy-five hundred feet above sea level, the bitter cold was alleviated only by reassurance that she was no longer alone. During the day, after Bob went to work, we often went to his house to eat. Every time Hattie and Bob's dog, Mutt, would bark I was up and searching. I was becoming so physically exhausted I was mentally spaced out. Since Bob had no bathroom, or even running water, we still could not bathe. I prayed that this primitive living would not harm our unborn baby.

On the television show, John Walsh said Betsy was believed to be seven or eight months pregnant. I often wondered if he was capable of feeling any compassion for a hunted pregnant woman who had committed no crime. I tried to feel compassion for him by remembering that the tragic murder of his son originally motivated him to become such a zealot with his sensationalistic expose'. Nevertheless, I was upset that he charged me with an armed robbery I did not commit, and I was very concerned about how it might affect my wife and unborn child.

After a week in the tent, Betsy and I were becoming exhausted and stir-crazy. At least twelve times each twenty-four hours I would scout both the cabin and the house, during which I memorized every tree and rock on the premises. With nerves on edge, bitter cold, dirty grime, and interrupted sleep, we eventually suffered a type of battle fatigue.

Relief came in the form of a silly remark one of us made that produced laughter. The more we laughed the more our laughter increased, until we nearly lost control. Hattie, with her ears straight up, looked at us with great perplexity, tilting her head from one side to the other. Her comical behavior only produced additional laughter. We needed just such an emotional catharsis; we felt emotionally purged afterward and were able to think more clearly. Since we saw absolutely no signs of anything amiss, and since there had been no suspicious calls on the police scanner, we decided to return to the cabin.

Assessing all the facts, I concluded that no one in New Mexico had recognized us from television, due largely to our extreme caution. When I had ordered building materials I always did it over the phone and paid the driver in cash. Every time a driver saw me I was wearing a hat and sunglasses, and unlike the picture on TV, I was clean shaven. Other people on the mountain either had no television at all, had no satellite dish to pick up this channel, or would not choose to watch "America's Most Wanted." Furthermore, most of the people on the mountain who knew us were attending a party when the program was aired. It did indeed seem that God personally arranged all the events to delay my capture until it was in compliance with his redemptive plans.

I decided to test the waters by walking down the road to the cabin in such a manner that I could be clearly seen. Then I went to see Debbie and Ray to see if I could detect any suspicious behavior by them. I told them we had been to Sante Fe for a week.

Since everything seemed to be okay, we cautiously returned to the cabin. We made an elaborate escape route through the back window, and I set up warning signals around the back yard.

The second night a car with bright lights came speeding down a dirt road which dead-ended on our road. If anyone crossed our road they would continue into our driveway, which they did. Because they were speeding, and because the downhill slope added to their momentum, they slammed on brakes and slid a long distance into our driveway. Their bright head lights lit up the inside of our cabin like spotlights, and Hattie was immediately up, barking.

I flew out of bed, still half asleep, screaming orders to Betsy and grabbing clothes we purposely left out in case of sudden flight. I ran to the window, sliding it open and throwing two emergency bags out the window and putting a thick blanket over the sill to make the crawl easier for Betsy. I jumped out first in case someone might be there. Then Betsy climbed through, big belly and all. Suddenly I noticed the cabin again grow dark as the car had backed out of our driveway. I went to the edge of the house to see it sputtering down the road and heard the loud drunken cursing of its occupants.

My heart was pounding in my ears as I turned to see Betsy crying. I took her in my arms and tried to soothe her, but I knew how badly she needed to cry; the pressure had finally reached its limit and the dam had broken loose. It was not until we were back in the cabin and in bed that Betsy, still in my arms, cried herself to sleep. This harrowing experience took its toll, and the adrenalin continued pumping in my veins so profusely I could not return to sleep. Hattie also was edgy, looking up at me every time I moved. "It's okay, Hattie," I whispered; "it's okay." And I said a silent prayer that it would indeed be okay.

After that terrible night I knew I must force myself to stay calm for Betsy's sake, seeking to make her as comfortable and secure as possible. If I saw or heard anything suspicious, I acted very nonchalant until I could investigate. After two weeks, we were almost back to normal. "That's just what they'd want us to do," I thought to myself with paranoia. Despite the apparent calm, I investigated everything that could be construed as suspicious, even though Betsy did not realize it. It was not till several years later, after counseling with Dr. Floyd and after Betsy's 1996 studies in college psychology, that we understood these episodes as the precipitating events that produced our lingering post traumatic stress disorder (P.T.S.D.).

As a result of such oppressive stress, Betsy and I sometimes broke into heated arguments over irrelevant things, but soon recovered, hugging each other tightly, whispering apologies and declarations of "I love you." Most of the time these flare-ups followed phone calls to relatives who transmitted all kinds of awful reports. Many of these reports originated with my old friend Sonny, who blamed me for the troubles he had created for himself through excessive use of alcohol and drugs.

Meanwhile, things in Virginia were going badly. Of particular pain was the situation with Betsy's mother, who feared she would forfeit her forty thousand dollars bond money paid for Betsy's release. We didn't blame her for being upset and we felt terrible guilt about it. We vowed we would somehow pay her back, no matter how long it took. We hoped Betsy's wealthy stepfather would help Betsy's mother (as he often did) so that she did not suffer financial deprivation.

Betsy's bond was initially set inordinately high because of the financial reputation of her wealthy stepfather, Mr. Kabler, and the false assumption that she too was rich. Because of Faye Johnson, the sensationalist newspaper reporter, Betsy became known as "the little rich girl"; the idea of Betsy having money made the authorities all the more hostile toward her.

It was true that Mr. Kabler had paid her college expenses and occasionally provided small sums of spending money during her college days, but Betsy's finances were very limited and her lifestyle quite frugal. Mr. Kabler did help Betsy with legal expenses but that was as far as it went. She had no part in his estate whatsoever, since he and Betsy's mother had long ago been divorced.

My family also developed antagonistic feelings toward us. Considering all the embarrassment my notoriety had caused, I couldn't blame them; the stories embarrassed me as well. Every time we called home we heard news of yet another derogatory article. The newspapers printed stories that were often sheer fabrications, designed to maintain public interest when the trail was cold. Hearing nothing of us, reporters even wrote about that. One article stated, "The trail is cold," and another, "They seem to have dropped off the planet."

More than a third of the printed stories were at least one-quarter false, completely dissecting my life from early childhood, and ruthlessly disparaging our families, friends, and associates. Because the newspaper distortions left our families depressed and demeaned, our telephone conversations with them depressed Betsy and me as well. And because we needed as much peace as possible, we decided to stop calling any of them. We missed everyone and worried about them, but it just wasn't worth the hassle to call; it didn't help anyone, and it only caused hurt and anxiety.

Within a month after the second television showing we were back to normal. We determined to finish the house as soon as possible. We wanted to sell it and head deeper into the wilderness to minimize contact with people. We decided to buy a piece of property in the mountains of Colorado, Northern New Mexico, or Arizona, in an area where there wasn't even any electricity. We needed a safe place to relax.

Before getting the loan on our new house, we found ourselves down to our last fifty cents. We hadn't paid the midwife and she had already given Betsy extensive prenatal care. In New Mexico midwifery and home births are legal. Barbara, a licensed, experienced practitioner, was our friend, but we could not abuse her friendship by neglecting to pay her. We therefore decided to sell our car to pay her fees and have something left for our personal needs. We cleaned it thoroughly, fixed all the obvious flaws, and placed ads in the local paper. After a week, we sold it for twenty-four hundred dollars. Having originally bought it for much less, we were pleased with the service it had provided and the profit it produced.

Now we were stuck with the International Scout for primary transportation. We were hesitant to drive the Dodge truck, lest the police might spot it. I didn't believe they would have the license number, and based on that false assumption, I occasionally drove it into town to pick up building materials.

Our twelve-thousand dollar home loan was finally approved at 16% interest, a reasonable rate for people in our poor circumstances. Our payments were three hundred dollars a month for five years, more like a car payment than a house payment.

We were nearing completion on construction of the house. The entire house was dried in, with 90% of the siding done, all the windows and doors hung and the roof finished. I believed I could finish it for around ten–thousand dollars. With the sale of the car and the loan, we felt confident we could make it. We owed the midwife about eight–hundred dollars, which would leave two thousand dollars till we could sell the house. After completing the house we could always get a fifteen year mortgage, provide the money to pay off the twelve-thousand dollar loan, and still have enough to live on while selling the house. That was the plan.

We believed the house would sell quickly, considering all the favorable comments we had received about it. We designed it with the look of a mountain house, featuring a cathedral ceiling and exposed beams. Part of the second floor was a loft that overlooked the first floor living room. The floors were all two by six inch tongue in groove spruce, framed with two-by-six-inch beams instead of two by fours to accommodate R-19 insulation.

The back of the house had numerous windows facing south for a passive solar effect, and all the major appliances, such as stove and water heater, would be gas. It had two bedrooms and a large study that could be used as another bedroom or nursery. It was simple and small, but everyone seemed to like it. And it was probably the cheapest house ever built. With a home owner's permit I did everything except the gas lines, the well, and septic tank. And I didn't buy anything without getting three prices and a discount for paying cash.

There was always work to be done within and around the house, even when we were broke. There were things like blocking between studs, soffit work, trim work around doors, windows, and corners, plus lots of landscaping. Our acreage was full of rocks which I moved to form a driveway, carved out of the wilderness. The driveway was about one hundred feet long and curved in such a way that the house could hardly be seen from the road.

Every day I worked until nightfall and sometimes later, using a drop cord for lighting. Looking back now, I believe I was having a paternal "nesting syndrome," preparing a place for our baby. It was at this time I realized how greatly my attitude had changed since the previous births of my two daughters, Robin Michelle and Joyce, January 10, 1968, and January 2, 1969, during my first marriage. I was always concerned for my first wife during her pregnancies, yet the spiritual dimension was absent back then. The anticipation of this new life produced a Godly excitement because I now knew the Giver of life in all His wondrous creativity. The marvelous love Betsy and I felt for each other and for our unborn child was sanctified by and within a superior love above and beyond our own—the redemptive love of a forgiving Savior.

The vast contrast in my anticipated fatherhood during the 1960s on the one hand, and the 1970s on the other, highlighted an amazing paradox. During my first marriage I was in the throes of my rebellious attitude and irresponsible behavior, living in bondage to self-centeredness, self-doubt, and lack of any ultimate purpose in life. Now, as a fugitive, hunted throughout the entire nation, my fears were counterbalanced by awareness that no matter what might transpire in today's human drama, the divine drama of the Cross permeated my redeemed life in such a way that I could say with St. Paul, *"I have learned in whatsoever state I am, therewith to be content...whether well fed or hungry, whether living in plenty or in want. I can do all things through Christ who strengthens me"* (Philippians 4:11-13).

Above all else, my primary concern was for Betsy and the baby. I could endure arrest and imprisonment for anything I had or had not done as long as I knew Betsy and our child would be well cared for. In the meantime, we prayerfully claimed the promise of Isaiah: *"Thou wilt keep him in perfect peace whose mind is stayed on thee, because he trusteth in thee"* (Isaiah 26:3).

Close to the expected delivery date Betsy acquired a terrible cold. A month had passed since our stay in the woods, yet this malady must have been a kind of delayed reaction. The worst part was that she could not take medication because of her pregnancy, not even something to help obtain her much-needed sleep. As she spent most of the night coughing and blowing her nose, the baby was kicking and moving around; when the baby calmed down her coughing started all over again. None of the herbal teas or soups or large doses of vitamin C seemed to help; Betsy was truly miserable! I finally took her to town to see a doctor who prescribed appropriate antibiotics and cough syrup that would be safe for the baby.

As she recuperated, I then caught her cold, which became the worst and longest I ever had. Our physical resistance had been thoroughly depleted by all the craziness of the past two months, by agonizing stress, and by physical over-exertion. The closer Betsy came to the delivery date, the more I stayed home with her. We had always used two-way radios while I worked on the house and she was in the cabin, but now I felt a need to be there with her. Betsy began cleaning the house and preparing everything for the birth. She even prepared several days' meals in advance.

In late March, halfway into her eighth month of pregnancy, Debbie and Ray organized several couples who lived near us. Together with Barbara, our midwife, "Junk Yard Bob," and others, they planned to give Betsy a surprise shower. Not limited to couples alone, it included almost everyone on the mountain, children and all; it was a wonderful event. Because most of them were parents, they knew the things we would be needing: diapers, diaper pails, infant clothes, cleaning materials, pajamas, and all kinds of infant paraphernalia. They set it up under pretense of having dinner with Debbie and Ray. When we opened the door, twenty people yelled, "Surprise!" Betsy was so overwhelmed and touched she wept.

The shower brought us great joy. Away from family and friends and unable to let them know where we were, we felt we had no one with whom to share the joy of our anticipated child. But now we had these wonderful new friends who blessed us just as our families would have back home in Virginia.

The people we met in New Mexico were different from any others anywhere else. I once told Betsy that the Spirit of God must roam more actively at high altitudes to produce such good people. They were always kind and helpful yet never intrusive. They didn't ask about the past and were never nosey; they cared only how newcomers behaved while in their community. It seemed to be an inherited attitude from pioneering days when so many settlers of the "Wild West" were running from past mistakes in search of a new beginning. It was gratifying the way these people were so stable, laid back, dependable, and caring.

As the expected date drew near, Barbara visited Betsy more often, checking her vital signs and the position of the baby. On every trip she left important items that would soon be needed: sterilized cloth, gloves, alcohol, cotton swabs, olive oil, ball syringe, pads, more pillows, and expendable plastic covers for the bed. She also brought a bottle of oxygen in case of emergency.

Betsy and I were getting nervous but exhilarated. We were both tired of the pregnancy and ready for a baby. Finally, on that Sunday night I'll never forget, April 16, after our routine watching of *America's Most Wanted*, Betsy went into labor. We had been preparing ourselves for months, but suddenly I was near panic. I wondered if this home birth procedure was such a good idea. If something went wrong, the closest hospital was over thirty miles away, down winding mountain roads. After further reflection and prayer, however, we dug in our heels, ready for whatever was to happen.

For several hours Betsy had painful contractions every fifteen or twenty minutes. Then, around ten-thirty or eleven, soon after Barbara arrived, the contractions became more frequent and more painful. By midnight Betsy was screaming and I was doing all I could to comfort her. I held her, gently massaging her shoulders, back, and neck; I wiped her face with a damp cloth.

Coral, Barbara's partner, showed up about eleven-thirty, by which time Betsy was experiencing serious pushing with great pain, interspersed with screams. When the contractions came, with her arms around my neck, she pulled my head with such force I thought she would choke me. She squeezed my arm so tight it produced numerous bruises seen the next day.

Betsy could not find relief in her travail. At one point she was on the bathroom floor pushing her feet against the wall, almost through the wall. Then she was back in bed, then on the floor. At midnight Debbie came over to help "coach." Her experience and reassuring manner provided great comfort. Since she had been through it five months earlier, she knew what it was all about.

Between contractions I pried myself loose from Betsy's grip and ran to the refrigerator to gulp down a cold drink. I was soaked from sweat. Then I restoked the fire in the fireplace. Betsy's prolonged travail was taking a terrible toll. Only her exhaustion prevented her from recognizing the gravity of her condition. I kept telling her she was doing good, which was true in light of her pain. I was tremendously impressed with the remarkable strength and courage of this amazing woman, my wife.

Barbara was worried because Betsy's water hadn't broken yet. When I realized what she was about to do, I was gripped by foreboding. The midwives told stories of jittery husbands who became so distraught that they only got in the way and made things worse. Remembering such stories, I forced myself to trust them and stay out of their way. But when Barbara produced this long thin instrument with a sharp edge on one end and told us what she was going to do, I almost panicked. The instrument was to be inserted up into the womb to puncture the placenta that enveloped the baby. I protested, but finally agreed to let them proceed, giving them a look that said, "We all die if you fail." Fortunately, it worked; the placenta was punctured, the water broke. But the baby still didn't move.

After this, either Barbara or Coral constantly had her gloved hand up the birthing canal, saying she could feel the baby's head, or saying the baby was crowning or something else encouraging. They told Betsy she would have to push harder as the baby was coming. At three in the morning I was elated to hear Barbara say again that the baby was coming, only to have my hopes dashed when it did not happen. They must have said it over twenty times, but nothing happened. Betsy was terribly exhausted, and I felt overwhelmed with vicarious exhaustion. How much longer could this go on?

Eventually, I asked Betsy if she wanted me to take her to the hospital. She was crying, sobbing, and sometimes screaming. Both of us said many desperate prayers for mercy and deliverance. I was ready to admit that I was scared to the depth of my being, and thoroughly humbled.

Later, around 3:00 a.m., Barbara decided she would have to perform an episiotomy, cutting vulva tissue to allow more room for the baby to pass. Betsy screamed so loud it made my ears ring, and the sight of her blood really had me distraught; the bleeding was profuse. Both midwives had been saying for hours that the baby was coming, and I no longer believed either of them. My feelings of fear and apprehension slowly gave way to anger. I asked Betsy again if she wanted me to take her to the hospital, and when she said, "Maybe, if it doesn't come soon," I knew she too was getting desperate.

Finally, at 4:05 a.m., after a giant push, we could see the top of the baby's head. I got very excited, and with new gusto I told Betsy the baby really was coming: "I saw it with my own two eyes." She looked up at me, her face all sweaty, her eyes wet with tears, and asked, "Really?" as if refusing to be misled by any more false reports. She wanted the truth! "Yes," I said, "the baby is really coming; push hard." With renewed strength she began to push again and the entire baby's head came out.

Nothing had prepared me for this. It was truly awesome. No, it was incredible! I was expecting a little doll-size baby, but this child was huge and real and moving (thank God!). Overwhelmed, my eyes as big as saucers, I hollered, "Push Bets!" And again: "PUSH!" We knew that deliverance was finally at hand, and Betsy exerted renewed determination. With an ear-shattering scream, wonder of wonders, our little son was there—all the way!

The midwife held our baby in both her hands, placing the child on Betsy's stomach, and instructing me to hold the baby there so she could quickly clean out the mouth. Another wave of panic swept over me as I saw no sign of breathing. When I turned the baby on its side Barbara cleared his mouth with the rubber syringe and the baby began to breathe and gurgle and cough and sputter. Then I too allowed myself to breathe a sigh of relief. In the subsequent calm, it seemed that all sound had disappeared from my ears and all activity reverted to slow motion. Then, the moment the baby began to breathe regularly, I heard Betsy exclaim; "It's a boy! The Lord gave us a boy!" It amazed me how quickly her agony was replaced by a calm, unbounding joy.

Barbara put the surgical clamps on the umbilical cord and I cut it. We laid him on Betsy's breast where he immediately began to nurse. I have heard that babies born by natural childbirth are much more alert than those from sedated mothers, and I can believe it. I also read that the practice of taking the baby from the mother immediately after birth and placing it in the nursery is an unsettling emotional deprivation for a newborn. Instead, the baby needs to stay close to the mother's body where he had developed during nine months gestation, where the mother's heart beat and warmth had sustained him both physically and emotionally.

The overwhelming trauma of the entire experience was so intense I could no longer hold back the tears. My tears expressed joy, relief, and gratitude for the experience of witnessing such a miracle. Betsy too was crying and smiling at the same time. The Scripture of John 16:21 came to my mind in those moments: "A woman giving birth to a child has pain because her time has come, but when her child is born she forgets the anguish because of her joy that a child is born into the world."

It was truly amazing that Betsy, who had been screaming in agony just minutes before, was now smiling, talking, and crying with happiness, holding her baby, her son, and listening with ecstasy to the noises he was making. Whereas he appeared huge when just half born, he now seemed very petite. He was incredibly active, with little arms and legs moving in every direction. Opening and closing his eyes, he would wrinkle his face and look like he had just awakened.

After cleaning the room, I also washed myself, put on a clean shirt, and took the baby so that Barbara and Coral could begin the tedious job of Betsy's surgical reconstruction. The flashlight Barbara had ordered the day before was now employed effectively; Coral held the light while Barbara stitched.

Other than some antiseptic spray that contained novocain, Betsy had received nothing for pain. I could tell that her pain was tremendous, yet she dealt with it magnificently. I was proud of her beyond words.

I lay down with our son on my chest, with his head cuddled in my neck and under my chin. I could hear him making a variety of delicate noises and it was music to my ears. I could feel his contentment, and I beamed with happiness. I whispered to him, "I love you, my son." Soon thereafter, I returned him to Betsy's breast, where he immediately resumed nursing.

I re-stoked the fire in the fireplace, as one of us had been doing all night long. Debbie had gone home as exhausted as the rest of us. Then Coral, Barbara, and I raided the refrigerator. Betsy had thoughtfully prepared all kinds of sandwiches and snacks the day before, in anticipation of this occasion. I had been so caught up in Betsy's delivery I had forgotten that Barbara's children, Jeffrey and Aimee, had been in the loft the whole time. Although fast asleep at that moment, I felt sure they now knew that the stork did not bring this baby.

Five-year-old Jeffrey and nine-year-old Aimee were no strangers to our cabin. Betsy and I had often kept them while Barbara was away attending to some other mother-to-be. We were very fond of them and my heart especially went out to Aimee, who had never known her father.

Hattie also had a terrible night, whining in vicarious trauma with every cry Betsy made. Now she was sleeping peacefully in her little corner of the cabin. The poor dog never knew what to expect next from us.

Around ten in the morning everyone finally left. Betsy and I were alone with our son whom we named Tucker Coleman. Tucker was the name of my youngest brother who had been so good to us, and Coleman was my mother's father, also nicknamed "Captain Rush" because he moved so quickly through the community, always in a hurry to help troubled people with their problems. We bundled up Tucker in a little blanket between us and drifted off to sleep watching him. Every fifteen minutes or so one of us would wake up to check on Tucker and make sure he was all right. Because I was so afraid I might roll over on him, I would not allow myself to sleep too soundly.

About every two hours he would wake up and I would change his diaper. Then I put him on Betsy's breast to nurse and on my chest to burp him. I soon learned that newborn babies don't burp very well, but they have no problem passing gas.

The rest of the day we catnapped and learned about baby care. I became increasingly proficient with the feeding. We felt confidence and satisfaction in our new parental roles.

The second day after the birth I ventured out of the cabin to work on the house. On my way through the newly charted path through the woods, I discovered Mutt and Hattie consummating their relationship. We knew Hattie had gone into heat but with all the excitement of Tucker's birth we neglected to separate them. And now it was too late. The family would now be bigger yet.

Returning home, I could see from the expression on Betsy's face that something was terribly wrong; Tucker was turning yellow with jaundice. I immediately called Barbara, and she decided we must take him to a physician in town. We all piled into Barbara's car and drove into Albuquerque to a private hospital with a highly skilled pediatrician.

The doctor was concerned, reporting that Tucker's bilirubin count was up to eighteen, and that a count of twenty-five could cause brain damage. Betsy and I were astounded, scared half to death. We checked him into the hospital where he was placed under bilirubin lights. The hospital staff allowed us to stay in the room with him, setting up a small bed for Betsy and a small cot for me. Little Tucker was placed in a clear plexiglass crib with eye patches to prevent the lights from damaging his eyes. We turned him over every hour or so. What sunlight provides for babies in the open, these bilirubin lights provide more evenly in the clinical setting.

I set the rocking chair where I could hold Betsy's hand and be close to the crib. We both fought back tears seeing him lie there with those big patches on his eyes. Upon waking, he would often hook a finger under the patch and try to pull it off. We fed him and changed him as we had done at home, with the hospital providing diapers and little blankets. We felt extremely helpless, yet deeply grateful for the fine care Tucker received. Nurses came in every four hours to prick his heel for blood and get a jaundice count. Because they knew we were waiting anxiously for the results, they always hurried back to report. Each time they gave us good news with compassion and encouragement.

In the morning the doctor came in to see us and examine Tucker. He said we were all doing well and that when the count dropped below thirteen we could all go home. That evening Barbara came and took us home. The following day I made a polyurethane tent on the front porch of the cabin enabling us to sit together in diffused sunlight, free from the chilly wind. That evening the yellow tint was almost gone and we began to receive visitors. Everyone who had been at the shower, and others, came by to see the baby and to bring gifts of food and drink.

It felt wonderful to have such warmth and affection from these fine people. Their affection was genuine, and out of consideration for Betsy and the baby, no one stayed too long. We loved those people dearly: Debbie and Ray, John and Marjie, Sonny and Jane, Bob, Barbara, our other fine neighbor, Mike and his son, Fred and Fanny, Tom and Mickel. They visited at different times, but always with good will in their hearts and happiness for us.

With Tucker's jaundice completely gone, I resumed building the house. At that point the framing inspection and the rough-in inspections were done. We felt great satisfaction with the progress of our creativity. We enjoyed each other to the fullest, as Betsy was slowly but surely recuperating. Those precious days are forever burnt into my heart and soul as a little bit of heaven here on earth, soon to be replaced by the bitterness of hell.

Eight days after Tucker was born we needed groceries and building materials. Because the clutch was almost worn out and the muffler had fallen off the Scout, I decided to drive the Dodge truck. I had a strange premonition that morning, a kind of eerie feeling. Before leaving, I asked Betsy to say a special prayer for me. She detected my apprehensive mood and asked me to be careful and to please hurry back.

I first stopped to pick up chimney pipe the building supplier had ordered for me. After purchasing the pipe, I drove up Ubank Boulevard, only to notice a police car in my rearview mirror several blocks back. I didn't think it was too unusual, since I had seen dozens of them behind me at one time or another. Even when his red light came on I assumed that he must have just received a call and was responding. But then I felt an icy chill as he continued following instead of passing me.

I approached a line of cars backed up from the red light at the intersection and realized I had no place to go and no way to run. I was still hoping that his flashing red light was for someone else, but then I heard the shrill, penetrating loud speaker of the police cruiser: "You in the white truck, come out of your vehicle with your hands on top of your head." I looked around for another white truck, but there was none; he was definitely talking to me.

I was in the worst possible position to run, trapped in the traffic with no outlet. Then the policeman was out of his car, pointing a gun at me with hands that appeared very shaky.

When several more police cars came roaring up and police bailed out brandishing their guns, I quickly realized he had radioed for back-up. In just a few seconds they had me out of the truck, down on my knees, hands on top of my head, in the middle of the street.

The policeman had run a check on my tag when he passed me the first time, before I even went in the store. He later told me he was suspicious of a Florida tag in New Mexico. The message that came back on his computer read: "SUSPECTED FUGITIVE MAY BE OPERATING THIS VEHICLE; CONSIDERED ARMED AND EXTREMELY DANGEROUS; NOTIFY FBI IMMEDIATELY." I persisted in my claim that I was Wayne Crews, with plenty of legitimate ID to prove it, but they were not about to let me go without checking fingerprints and notifying the Feds.

In a very real sense, the period of time between our conversion in Charlotte, North Carolina, October 7, 1988, and my recapture in New Mexico, April 26, 1989, was for Betsy and me like the children of Israel wandering in the wilderness. Whereas their exodus from Egyptian bondage was the result of divine deliverance, and my escape from the Port City Jail resulted from my own intrigue, the end result was escape and freedom in both instances. As their redemptive relationship with God was established through covenant commitment in the Passover celebration of Egypt, so our redemption was established in new covenant commitment to Christ on the road to Charlotte and in the Red Roof Motel on Billy Graham Boulevard. In both cases, God provided redemptive power by His unique intervention. We stumbling creatures of clay merely responded with imperfect faith to His provision of life and freedom.

Like the Israelites of old, Betsy and I were also babes in the wilderness who needed to grow spiritually. We had no understanding of discipleship and we had much to learn, yet we had attempted to live under the lordship of Christ while wandering in our wilderness of New Mexico.

Whereas the Israelites concluded their wilderness wandering with a victorious march into the Promised Land, ours ended with heart-rending recapture. God taught us hard discipleship through a humane Babylonian captivity in New Mexico and a cruel Assyrian captivity in South Carolina and Port City, Virginia. Only after we had endured the bleak days of separation and prison at Powhatan did God graciously provide reunion and entrance into the Promised Land of His freedom in a unique manner beyond our wildest imagination.

CHAPTER 8

BABYLONIAN CAPTIVITY
JAIL IN NEW MEXICO

Terror and desperation struck me all at once when I thought of Betsy and Tucker up in the mountains alone, needing me more than ever. I tried to remember if there was anything in my wallet or in the truck that could possibly lead police to the cabin. All my ID had the Albuquerque address of our previous apartment. There were warrants out for Betsy too. If they arrested her, they would surely take our child. I prayed intensely for their safety and that I could somehow get word to Betsy.

Within an hour I was in the Albuquerque jail being fingerprinted and photographed. I was screaming to God inside, begging that He would let this be just a dream. As soon as I got to the jail, I asked to use the phone to call a lawyer. After removing the cuffs, they pointed me to a phone.

I called Debbie and Ray's number, saying a silent prayer that one of them would be home. Ray answered on the second ring. I fought to control my shaky voice as I told him I didn't have time to explain, but I needed him to do something for me that was of life-and-death importance. At that moment I noticed an FBI agent at the front counter looking for the suspected fugitive. I hurriedly told Ray to go get my wife and baby and put them on a plane back East immediately. As the agent rushed toward me I hung up the receiver.

He took my wallet and belongings from the police and began going through them. When he demanded to know the whereabouts of my wife I denied having a wife and claimed my name was Wayne Crews, not Robert Witt. As soon as he left I grabbed the phone again and called the first lawyer I found in the yellow pages.

The first lawyer answered and I soon realized that he was not the one I needed. I said, "Listen, I'm in a critical situation and other people's lives are at stake, and I need a real lawyer and I need him fast."

There was a short pause in which I was afraid he was going to hang up; then he said, "Hold on a second." He was back in less than a minute with the name and number of another lawyer, Roger A. Finzel. I tried with all my determination to remember the number as I hung up and redialed. Thank God, Finzel answered and within two minutes I knew I had the right man, a real lawyer.

I briefly told him of my situation, emphasizing that my wife was in danger. Because neither of us trusted the phone, we talked in riddles and I gave him the number of someone back East to coordinate retrieving Betsy and the baby. He did not then know that Betsy was also wanted.

Betsy and I had often rehearsed potential scenarios of capture, assuming that it would probably be me rather than Betsy. We made plans for each eventuality and kept a stash of four hundred dollars we would never touch for any reason other than what was happening now. The money would be enough for a plane ticket to one of several places where we knew we could count on someone for help. I hoped with all my heart that Betsy and the baby had made it out of New Mexico safely.

Although Debbie and Ray were very curious about what was happening, they never asked any questions. I later learned they had given Betsy the message. She was terribly upset, but faithfully executed our plans. In the morning, enormous relief swept over me as I learned that Betsy, Tucker, and even Hattie had made it to the East Coast and were there with family. Thank God! That was a tremendous load off my mind.

Roger Finzel was an outstanding lawyer who had once been on the defense team for the famous Wounded Knee trials of the early '70s. He was one of the few lawyers I could really appreciate for both the quality of his character and his professional competence. The following morning, he and I were in district court facing half a dozen media people with cameras, microphones, and questions. An agent from *America's Most Wanted* was there trying to claim credit for the capture. They still falsely claim me as one of their success stories, even though my capture was actually due to a routine traffic check by an alert young police rookie who never saw me on television. He was merely curious about my Florida tags.

Because the Commonwealth Attorney in Port City, Virginia, submitted reports that were greatly exaggerated, bail was set at half a million dollars. New Mexico authorities treated this as much more than a routine apprehension of a common fugitive. The Virginia papers headlined: *"Witt Caught, Wife Still Missing."* Subsequent articles became even more sensational, as did the craziness that was to follow. Thus began my relatively brief incarceration in New Mexico, dubbed "The Babylonian Captivity."

The jail in Albuquerque was different from any jail I had ever seen: it had no bars. Each block was enclosed in glass and each cell had a steel door with an oblong window about five inches by twenty inches. The cells were twice the size of any jail cell I had ever seen, each with a window that allowed inmates to see outside. Compared with the dungeons of Kulumbah, South Carolina, and Port City, Virginia, this was absolutely humane. What a privilege to be so close to daylight!

There was also a table and bench in each cell, another comfort I had never seen in Virginia jails. The most amazing thing of all was the encased light on the wall that could be controlled by the inmate. At night I could actually turn off the light and be in total darkness, something very precious to anyone who has ever been subjected to bright lights twenty-four hours a day, as is done in most detention centers. It was also air-conditioned and served the best meals I've ever eaten in confinement.

Twice a day all prisoners were let out of their cells for a half hour to make phone calls and take showers. They even had an exercise machine inmates could use. Most of the residents were Chicanos, the best people I've ever done time with. They seemed to have more moral scruples than other criminals I have known. If I had to be in jail, I would prefer this one in New Mexico, perhaps the most enlightened and most humane jail in the country.

Although the comforts of this amazing new jail were very pleasant, my inner feelings were unaffected. I felt like the end of my world had come, yet with emotional pain instead of death. All I could think about was my wife and son, and what lay ahead. I kept wondering how I could get out of this jail, back to Betsy and Tucker before they ran out of money or got into trouble.

I heard that the authorities in Kulumbah, South Carolina, wanted me as a robbery suspect there. Instinct told me the Feds had something to do with that charge, since they believed I had committed many unsolved federal crimes and they wanted convictions everywhere possible, just in case I might beat the Port City case. I later discovered that calls from viewers of *America's Most Wanted* accused me of numerous other crimes, but such charges were quickly dismissed after it was finally proven I had been elsewhere during the alleged crimes. In several cases police authorities had already caught the guilty parties.

Virginia authorities were putting out all kinds of mis-information. The Port City sheriff contacted New Mexico, telling them that I was a dangerous escape artist. The New Mexico authorities responded by ordering me shackled when outside my cell, and having my cell checked every fifteen minutes while I was in it. Guards wearied themselves walking by my cell.

I desperately wanted to hear from Betsy that she was safe and well. I could not think of her and my infant son without getting a lump in my throat. I prayed they were safe and that Betsy was holding up emotionally. I had no idea where they were.

On my fourth day in captivity, while lying on my bunk staring up into nothingness, I heard a man singing. I could not at first recognize the song, but his voice was like medicine to my weary soul. When I got up and placed my ear to the door I recognized the beautiful refrain: "This is my story, this is my song, praising my Savior all the day long..."

Just as suddenly as it began, the singing was gone. I missed it terribly, even though I had no idea who the singer was. I did know it was not an inmate because it came from outside the cell block. Whoever it was, he had created a profound longing for more. Even though the singer did not have a professionally trained voice, it was truly inspiring. After that brief, uplifting interlude, however, my anxiety about Betsy and Tucker was accentuated even more. I prayed that night as never before. I wept and I prayed, "God, please protect my wife and son. And please help me..."

Several days later I heard the singing again, but this time a man appeared singing at my door. For a split second I wondered if he might be an angel who had come to take me away. His face was so full of love and joy that it became contagious. When he stopped singing he stood smiling through the narrow window. When he spoke, my heart almost jumped out of my chest. He said he was the jail chaplain and asked me how I was doing. From my silence and the expression on my face he must have thought I was deranged. Since I was afraid that if I talked I might break, with such a lump in my throat, I just nodded to him and he moved on respectfully.

A week later he came back and I learned that his name was Glenn Riddle. I told him my experience with Ricochet, the truck driver. I told him how my wife and I accepted Christ as Savior that same day. I went on to tell him all that had happened since then. I think he understood better than I did at the time how bitter I was toward God and all society for all my troubles. After he prayed with me and left, I didn't feel quite so isolated and hopeless as before.

The next day I called home and finally received what I had been waiting for: A telephone number to Betsy or to someone who could get through to her. I dialed the number, fearing that the line would be busy or the connection faulty. Someone answered and put me through to another line in case the police were tracing my calls. Then I heard Betsy's voice on the line. "RC, RC, are you there? Are you okay?"

I had a hard time answering, but finally heard my trembling voice answer, "Yes, Babe. Are you and the baby okay?" Then she was the one who could not answer. I could hear her sobbing, but she pulled herself together enough to talk. We both tried to reassure each other that each was okay. She told me the baby was fine and that she had flown Hattie to North Fork where a friend picked her up and carried her to my parents' house out in the country. Betsy told me she loved me and that I must have faith that things would somehow work out. She reminded me of the prayers we said our last morning together and said that God had a hand in this and was going to help us. She kept trying to encourage me and reassure me that she and Tucker were fine. Our time was up and we ended our call by making arrangements of time and place for the next call, declaring over and over again how much we loved each other.

Betsy and I were so tuned to each other when it came to communicating over suspicious phone lines we could say all kinds of cryptic things that would take a listener a month of Sundays to decipher. And it would be nearly impossible to trace our calls the way we arranged them.

At this point the Feds had obtained an "Interstate Flight to Avoid Prosecution Warrant" for her arrest, so we could not be too careful. Authorities posted her picture all over the jail and courthouse, believing she might try to get in to see me or even arrange my escape. Port City authorities again released exaggerated information about us, and this caused us great suffering. In order to have me featured on *America's Most Wanted*, and listed among the FBI.'s Most Wanted, the Port City Sheriff falsely reported that I was armed, violent, and suspected of murdering court witnesses. This report was issued without factual basis; I never owned or even carried a gun except in the Marine Corps. The Port City authorities knew that I was in prison when the witnesses were murdered and that I have neither committed nor ever been accused of committing *any act of violence* against anyone anywhere at any time.

Members of my family received several reports that my life would be in danger once I was back in the custody of Port City. The sheriff called the Albuquerque jail, asking when he could come get me. My lawyer and officers of the court expressed surprise at this unusual procedure. My lawyer decided it would be best to bring this matter out in the open as much as possible to prevent any harm to me. The best way to do this was by fighting extradition with a plea to the governor of New Mexico to recognize the danger and launch an investigation.

The Port City sheriff and prosecutors accused me of buying time to either escape or somehow avoid return to Virginia. The sheriff took the unusual action of calling the governor's offices of both Virginia and New Mexico. This we knew because someone in the New Mexico governor's office called my lawyer. I didn't really believe I was in that much danger until I kept hearing of Port City's mad zeal to come get me. I couldn't figure it out. I have never heard of a sheriff so upset over any escapee that he personally sought to go retrieve him across the continent. That isn't done even when escapes are violent and life-threatening, which mine were not. I never posed any danger to anyone, nor had I caused any damage during my escape.

I did recognize that my escape exposed the lax operation of the Port City jail and that was embarrassing to the sheriff. The jail facility itself was designed and constructed with good physical security and equipment such as cameras and electric locks; it was the lax procedures and personnel management that left so much to be desired and enabled me to escape the way I did. Evidently, my walking out of his jail was viewed as a personal affront that launched the sheriff on a never-ending vendetta against me.

In my previous sinfulness, I rationalized my deed as merely accepting the invitation provided by jail laxity to simply walk out. I also rationalized that the good citizens of Port City were fortunate that I was the one who took advantage of the weak spot rather than a crazed murderer bent on indiscriminant, sociopathic bloodshed. I realize now that my rationalization was a lame ego defense mechanism used to justify my sinful nature.

Every move my lawyer made was reported and sensationalized by the Virginia newspapers so as to rehash my escape and caricature my entire life through the use of exaggeration and falsehood. After receiving several letters in the form of mailograms from the reporter, Faye Johnson, I called her, hoping to get the feel of Port City public opinion. She said that the authorities wanted my wife as much as they wanted me, and the prosecutor referred to my wife as "the little rich girl," and felt that "the little rich girl" had pulled one over on them.

These printed exaggerations worried me greatly because such opinions were completely false on both counts. Betsy had never been rich or anything close to it, and she certainly had not pulled anything over on anyone. If anyone had pulled a fast one on anyone else it was the Port City Court which violated the written, signed agreement with Betsy, thus forcing her into a position where she had to either go to jail or run. I thought to myself, "What gall they have! She never did anything to warrant such deceit and duplicity!"

My wife's family hired a Port City lawyer, who went to the judge handling Betsy's case to get a feel for the court's attitude. The judge promised that if Betsy would turn herself in he would release her on bond to care for her new born baby. Knowing how treacherous Port City authorities had been, I would have told her not to do it.

When Betsy received the judge's promise, she left the baby with my mother, then seventy-two years old. Accompanied by her mother, she surrendered to the federal authorities in North Fork, thinking she would immediately be released to take care of the baby she was nursing. Instead, the Port City authorities again violated their solemn word and refused to grant Betsy bond at any price whatsoever.

Because of the hostility shown by the sheriff, Betsy told the chief magistrate she was afraid to go to the Port City jail, even overnight. The sheriff of a nearby county then agreed to accept Betsy in his jail. Because of the judge's promise, everyone thought Betsy would be in jail only a day or two at most.

When I called home the next day and learned what had happened, I was outraged. I was angry with everyone who encouraged Betsy to surrender: my family, her family, and especially her lawyer. Every time I called home I was told that the lawyer said he would have Betsy out in a week. We later learned that he never tried to get her out. I never could understand why he took the case at all, since one of his law partners was the lawyer for one of my co-defendants, Eddie Cantor, a seasoned criminal who never served a day for his part in the crime. He was given ten years probation long after Betsy's trial. One would assume conflict of interest when two lawyers of the same law firm defended both my wife and a man who gained undeserved probation by testifying against me.

Betsy was taken to jail and put in a cell block so over-crowded that as many women slept on the floor as in beds. Her breasts still produced milk as a constant reminder that her child needed her. Not only was our infant son going though the emotional shock of losing his mother, but he was suddenly deprived of his normal food supply. He initially refused his grandmother's bottle but was ulti-mately forced by hunger to take this new kind of nour-ishment. I often wonder what toll the trauma of that event took on the emotional development of our infant son.

I could not understand how Port City authorities could justify keeping Betsy locked up. The fact that she peacefully surrendered proved that she was not a risk, and I was already caught. Most importantly, it was inhu-mane to punish an infant less than two months old who had done no wrong. The lawyer claimed he sought the judge's permission to allow her to go to a hospital under guard to be with our child but that the judge denied his plea. Our families even offered to pay the cost. I was amazed that anyone could be so cruel.

Back in the Albuquerque jail, all the intense, pro-longed stress finally found expression in my physical health. The prostate problem flared up again and my stomach felt like it was full of broken glass. Because all simple, basic home health remedies ("first echelon maintenance") are impossible in jail, an inmate must mobilize inner resources to endure. I longed for relief in a tub of hot water, and I wished for the luxury of a visit to the corner drug store. Just a humanitarian attitude of caring and concern is healing in itself, but such is rarely found in jails.

After requesting medical help with my prostate trouble, days passed before I received even an aspirin, and several weeks before I could see a doctor. Jail authorities generally tend to think that inmates are always faking illnesses for one reason or another. They were even more suspicious of me because of my previous escapes and the warnings of Port City that I would try anything. When I finally saw a specialist, he took me to the hospital to have an obstruction removed from my urethra. This scar tissue could have come from the doctor who did the previous cystoscopy or it could have come from an old injury.

They put me under general anesthesia for an hour or so. Later, when I regained consciousness, I had a catheter about the size of my little finger draining my bladder into a bag full of bloody liquid. The guards would not help me dress, but left me in the hospital gown and put me in a wheel chair. I was still quite drowsy when the anesthesia began to wear off and felt increasingly severe pain.

The doctor had prescribed Perkaden for the pain and an antibiotic for prevention of any infection, but when I was returned to jail, guards refused to allow me anything more than super-strength Tylenol. No one instructed me on what to do with the bag, but once in the infirmary isolation cell I figured out that it had to be lower than my body and I fastened it on the bed.

I shall always remember with deep appreciation the kindness of a black lady who was on duty that night. She was the first person I saw, and she went out of her way to make me comfortable. Her kindness was like medicine to my soul as well as my body. Somehow she got me some stronger medicine and a large pitcher of juice with ice to help bring down my fever. Although most of the jail was comfortably air-conditioned, the uncooled infirmary cell felt like a furnace. This made the chilled juice all the more welcome. Her kindness accentuated the calloused indifference of the others. When, after four days, I could no longer stand the painful catheter, I pulled it out myself. It felt like I was pulling my intestines out through the penis, but once out, it was a big relief. I passed a great deal of blood immediately afterward, and it hurt to pass water for a long time. After a few days of recuperation, guards returned me to my regular cell.

During that time I was so constantly besieged with bad news about Betsy and our prosecution that I began to question God. I repeatedly cried out to Him, asking if He really cared about us. If so, why did He let all those terrible things happen? I knew Betsy was going through pure hell. Being away from her baby was agony enough all by itself, but dealing with the additional horrors of jail caused me to fear she might not withstand it all. I was afraid she might never again be the same. I was thankful to hear that my sister, Brooke, was regularly visiting Betsy in jail with the baby. Unfortunately, Betsy could only look at Tucker through a thick glass partition and vainly long to hold him.

My lawyer, Mr. Finzel, came to see me and reported that the governor had signed the extradition papers and would not consider an investigation. We decided that my best chance with South Carolina was to first obtain extradition there; an acquittal in South Carolina would later provide credibility in the Virginia trial. He therefore filed a habeas corpus to gain thirty days before Virginia could get me. Then I could waive extradition to South Carolina, thereby forcing South Carolina to come get me first.

We appeared in district court to get the thirty-day extension from Virginia and, at the same hearing, I waived extradition to South Carolina. The judge looked at my lawyer with a sly smile, as if to say, "Slick trick, Finzel." The judge had to grant fifteen days for South Carolina to get me, after which the detainer would automatically be dropped. Meanwhile, Virginia could do nothing for thirty days, by which time I would be in South Carolina.

Virginia newspapers dispensed word of this move, accusing me of "Avoiding Virginia Like the Plague," July 8, 1989. It was true that I was in no hurry to face Port City, but my first concern was to be exonerated in South Carolina before Port City could do their number on me.

Every time I called home my sister told me that Betsy's lawyer kept saying he would have her out in a week. He was beginning to remind me of the midwives who delivered our son, claiming for five hours that he was coming at any moment. For over a month Betsy was promised release "next week."

At one point Betsy's lawyer promised that he was going to the State Supreme Court to have her bond set. In actuality, he never even filed a motion in circuit court for any kind of bond. In my state of paranoid depression, it almost seemed that someone had spread the word that Betsy and I were fair game for victimization by anyone and everyone.

I wrote Betsy daily words of encouragement I did not always believe. I was confident she would be exonerated in her trial; I just tried to keep her hopes up until then.

When South Carolina came to get me I was still recuperating from the prostate surgery and was very weak. I had lost twenty pounds from a combination of the surgery and intense extended anxiety. I prayed that God would heal me and make the trip bearable. Thank God, we flew; a car trip would have been agonizing. There was an abundance of agony awaiting me in Kulumbah, South Carolina, a city I had never before visited. I identified numerous escape opportunities, but Betsy's incarceration and safety hung over me like a guillotine. If I had split, Port City would never have set her free with our baby. This was before I realized her lawyer had no intentions of getting her out anyway.

I received news that my friend, Sonny, had been convicted for aiding my escape. Because I had called him from the Port City jail and asked him to get Wilbur W. out on bond two-and-a-half years earlier, the jury convicted him of criminal conspiracy. The truth was that neither Sonny nor Betsy ever really knew what I was doing when I arranged Wilbur's bond. I was so naive I believed they would not be charged as long as they had no knowledge of my scheme. Sonny appealed and remained free on bond.

CHAPTER 9

ASSYRIAN CAPTIVITY
JAIL IN SOUTH CAROLINA

All these worries were abruptly, albeit not mercifully, interrupted upon my arrival in the city jail of Kulumbah. I really didn't believe places like this still existed. The building itself was old and dilapidated, and the jailers definitely belonged to a by-gone era of abuse.

Guards put me in a drunk tank about fifteen feet square. It already held a dozen men: drunks, druggies, and traffic violators. The tank was like a furnace, permeated by the oppressive East Coast humidity I had escaped while in New Mexico; it felt like I was breathing steam. There was one toilet in the corner that looked and smelled absolutely repulsive. The floor was caked with filth and there were steel benches on three walls.

The only thing I had sat on since my operation was a mattress, and then only long enough to eat or write a short letter. Sitting on steel for half an hour aggravated my prostate so severely I became truly ill. The entire cell was a combination of filthy steel and filthy cement.

Since there was no room on the benches to lie down and no floor space to walk around, I just stood still, hour after hour. As the night wore on, the police continued bringing in more prisoners, and the cell became even more unbearably crowded. I kept expecting them to transfer me from the drunk tank into a cell for long-term prisoners; unfortunately, that never happened.

After about eight hours I beckoned for a guard and tried to explain my health problem to him. He looked at me with a cold stare as if he didn't understand English. Since my operation, I had great difficulty passing water; I had to be totally relaxed. During my eight hours in this drunk tank I had not been able to pass water at all.

By this time my bladder was distended and painful, yet my kidneys simply would not release. Twice I stood at the toilet so long the others began to stare at me, causing me to self-consciously go back and look for a place to sit on the steel bench. I sat down and tried to shift my weight from one side to the other of my buttocks to relieve the pain in my prostate.

By six o'clock in the morning there were over twenty men crowded in the tank, one of the most disgusting spectacles I had ever seen. We were practically piled on top of each other. I still hadn't urinated and my bladder felt like it was going to burst. Surely they would put me in a cell block or a cell soon!

A few hours later they marched most of us over to bond court where the judge set a seventy-thousand-dol-lar bond. This was reasonable, I thought, considering my circumstances. Then, to my dismay, I was returned to that same damnable drunk tank. I had not slept for twenty-four hours and had been sweating profusely the whole time. During the day the July heat was stifling, and at night the tank seemed to hold the previous day's heat. I waited and waited and waited to be moved to a cell block where I could shower and lie down on a bed or at least a mattress, hoping that my kidneys would unlock. The pain in my bladder was excruciating. I was in total disbelief when another whole day again went by and I was still in that despicable tank. With more additions it totalled almost thirty men. I had never experienced anything like this before. After I begged one of the guards long enough, he let me out to use the long-distance phone. At three o'clock in the morning he escorted me down a hallway and locked me in a cage where the phones were located. I had not urinated for over thirty hours and had not slept in two days.

When my sister answered the phone I nearly wept. After talking with her I began to pull myself together. I gathered renewed strength from her reassuring words and her promise to call the local lawyer she had already hired. She promised to call him first thing in the morning.

After hanging up, while waiting for the guard to come back and get me, I suddenly urinated for the first time in nearly forty hours, right there on the floor. Although it was involuntary, the relief was so wonderful I didn't care what anyone might say. After all, what more could they possibly do to me? Put me in jail?

After staying in the tank most of that day, I was then moved to an overcrowded cell block just before supper time. I ate my first meal in over two days and took an invigorating shower. After assessing my new habitat, I lay down on my half-inch thick, well-worn pad of a mattress and slept for over twelve hours.

I was eventually awakened by some of the loudest noise I had ever heard in my life. My first reaction was to wonder how in the world I ever slept through it to begin with. The television was turned up to its highest volume and three black men were screaming at the top of their lungs at each other.

It seemed that most people in Kulumbah were still fighting the Civil War, with both blacks and whites the most racist I'd ever witnessed. In all fairness, I was forced to have empathy for the blacks when I realized that Kulumbah was predominantly white, yet four hundred and fifty of its five hundred jail inmates were black. Such statistics indicated that something was definitely out of kilter.

After a week I was finally able to see my lawyer. The first thing he told me was what a serious crime I was charged with, and that, because of my prior record, a celebrity *on America's Most Wanted*, the solicitor (prosecutor) was going to ask for a life sentence. When I protested, "But I didn't do it," he reacted with a cynical look as if to say: "Yeah, that's what they all say; don't insult my intelligence with that line."

My sister believed in my innocence because she knew I would never commit armed robbery. Betsy knew I was innocent because she was with me on September 2 and 3, and for a week thereafter, seven hundred miles away.

I had taken a polygraph exam in New Mexico, administered by one of the best criminal polygraph examiners in that part of the country. Mr. Finzel thought it would help with my fight against extradition, since it was admissible evidence in New Mexico. To warrant admissibility, New Mexico established strict procedures and validity standards; a prescribed score had to be attained for legal admissibility. Although the test score substantiated my claim of innocence, it was only one point above the required level for acceptance. Although South Carolina does not allow polygraph evidence in court, they will consider it in deciding whether or not to try a weak case. Because polygraph scoring in South Carolina is not as rigorous as in New Mexico, I felt I would easily pass it and thereby substantiate my innocence.

With the passage of time, my case in South Carolina looked increasingly grave. The police claimed that three credit union employees had identified me from a picture lineup. In light of this, I felt I needed help and asked to take the polygraph. The lawyer agreed but warned that the prosecution would try for a conviction if I failed it. I felt certain I would pass.

I was taken to the State Police Headquarters, where the test was administered by a uniformed officer, reputed to be a qualified examiner. When finished, he called the lawyer's assistant from the adjacent waiting room to report his findings.

I was so certain I would be exonerated I could hardly wait to say, "See, I told you guys I am innocent." Instead of relief and good news, however, I was flabbergasted to hear the alleged expert declare that I had lied on every question and that there was no doubt in his mind but that I was guilty. The awful truth gradually dawned on me that I had been set up, and it made me sick: sick with disgust and sick with fear. There was no longer any doubt in my mind that they were concocting an unjust case against me, and I had actually helped them by requesting the polygraph exam.

Later that night, when the lawyer came to see me at the jail, I told him what I thought and he told me I was wrong; he declared that he had known the examiner for years and he was a good man. He went on to say things

171

indicating that he himself believed I was guilty. Now also came the realization that I would be stuck in this awful jail for six or seven more months, possibly a year, before even going to trial.

This was one of the worst times of my entire life, probably the most disillusioning. I was being falsely accused of a serious crime that could easily get me a life sentence in the prison of another state, far from family and loved ones, without a single friendly face or encouraging word from anyone I knew.

During this terrible time God used two people to keep me from escape or suicide: my wife and my son. Thoughts of them kept me going day by day, but at night I covered my head and cried out to God over and over, "How could You let this happen?" I didn't know much about following Christ back then. I was to learn much later, but I must have been a terrible student for the Holy Spirit to deal with. I suppose He had to push me to such extremity to get my attention and render me teachable.

At my sister's insistence the lawyer hired a private investigator to research my whereabouts during the time of the robbery. He was Jim Tolbert, one of the best investigators I have ever known, and a truly fine, honest human being. When I first met him I did not like him because he also seemed to doubt my innocence. But he promised that he would produce the truth, one way or another. I hoped and prayed he would do so.

I had now been in the Kulumbah jail for almost a month. I spent my days either reading the Bible or writing Betsy words of encouragement that I really did not feel. She was four hundred miles away in her Virginia jail cell, with little hope among such hostile people. She was also doing the exact same thing, writing me words of encouragement that she didn't really feel. We cheered each other on during those terrible months, in spite of the appearance that we were both engulfed in losing battles.

In the midst of our trauma, my poor sister caught the brunt of our frustration. I am ashamed to admit that Betsy was much more patient and appreciative than I in dealing with my sister. I complained bitterly to her when I called. Betsy and I both called her regularly, conveying messages to each other through her. She was on the phone daily to lawyers, investigators, and others, helping in both our cases. She visited Betsy each week and took the baby every other week. All the while she held down a full-time job and managed her own family.

The investigator, through diligent research, came up with an enormous amount of irrefutable evidence proving my innocence, including details I myself had forgotten. On that September day in Florida I had been refurbishing houses for my employer, Dennis Burns. The houses were in Fort Myers, and I was living in Naples, both about seven hundred miles from South Carolina. Dennis kept records of everything, as did the builder's supply company. I had signed for materials picked up on that very day, and one company employee even remembered me.

Furthermore, it was on a Friday, and Dennis paid me by check. I cashed the check, and the bank recorded it on that day with my signature. From the bank I went to a rental store and rented a tow bar. They remembered because I kept the tow bar over a month.

Equally conclusive was the fact that the robber was clean shaven and I had a full beard. Many people saw me during that time with a full beard, including the minister and his assistant who married Betsy and me in Pensacola, six days after the robbery in South Carolina.

In addition to their verbal testimony, we had pictures of us standing on the steps at the wedding chapel. Because the average man's beard grows approximately half an inch per month, it was impossible for me to grow a full beard in six days. The City Hall clerk who issued our wedding license also saw me on Tuesday after the robbery with a full beard. After verifying the accuracy of the investigator's evidence, the solicitor dropped the charges.

I kept thinking about that polygraph examiner, who was a state policeman. I recalled his words that there was *no doubt in his mind* of my guilt. Could he have given me an honest test and my emotional condition thwarted the results? Possibly, but I truly doubt it. By his own statement, the machine was hardly ever wrong and never 100 percent wrong.

I finally concluded he willfully fabricated false evidence to help other police make a dishonest case, rationalizing that it was okay to burn me because I was undoubtedly guilty of some crimes, somewhere. Unfortunately, this type of immoral behavior by police officers was nothing new to me; I had experienced it many times before. I also reflected with pity on the poor devils who were unjustly accused, but had no family or money to hire a good lawyer and a fine investigator as my wonderful sister had done for me.

Citizens often think criminals go free due to lack of evidence, legal technicalities, or media hype, but this is usually not the case. It is a rare exception when a defendant gets off on a technicality or for lack of evidence. But when the evidence is as conclusive and as obvious as in my South Carolina case, the prosecution has no choice but to drop the case. They dropped charges against me on Thursday and I signed extradition on Friday.

The decision to waive extradition was a difficult one. On the one hand, resistance to extradition would have delayed return to Virginia for three months and enabled me to go free on bond during that time. On the other hand, such resistance would have further infuriated the Port City authorities and jeopardized the chances of Betsy's freedom; all family members and friends in Virginia warned against it for Betsy's sake. Faced with such a choice, I could not be selfish; I had to go back right away to support Betsy.

Just two days after I waived extradition, the Port City Sheriff, who claimed he had no personal prejudice, came to personally pick me up, together with his deputy sheriff. He had called the Kulumbah jail and requested that jail guards take me to the airport to meet them there.

I knew I was in trouble the minute they showed up. I had a grocery-size paper bag with my belongings in it: legal papers, personal hygiene items, and letters from Betsy. The sheriff demanded that I throw the bag away, and when I objected he snarled, "We ain't running no Holiday Inn." I pointed out that the bag contained my legal papers, whereupon he thought better of it and grudgingly let me keep the bag.

The Kulumbah deputies removed their handcuffs and the sheriff clamped his on my wrists—extra tight! Unlike the deputies who brought me from New Mexico to Kulumbah, the sheriff refused to take the cuffs off on the plane and refused to let me use the rest room except when we made a stop in North Carolina. Even then he ordered his assistant to stand in the doorway, breathing down my back.

With handcuffs on so tight my hands became numb, I tried unsuccessfully to relieve my bladder. I wouldn't have had time anyhow, since the sheriff soon barked orders for me to return to my seat. We never left the plane from Kulumbah, South Carolina, to North Fork, Virginia, and my overtaxed bladder was again painful.

All during the trip I kept thinking that the sheriff looked familiar, and it finally dawned on me who he was. He was one of the thirteen detectives on the burglary squad who had beaten me within an inch of my life after I had escaped their trap in the 1972 motorcycle shop stakeout. He was part of the crew that produced false witnesses, contradicted each other, and perjured themselves on the witness stand. He was an active member of the conspiracy that netted me three years in prison for an alleged crime that never even took place. His vendetta undoubtedly grew out of embarrassment, false pride, and loss of sleep on that night of police futility, seventeen years earlier.

The sheriff had informed all the news agencies, including his favorite reporter, Faye Johnson, of my return. He gave her the flight number, time of arrival, gate number, and his plan to escort me out the rear door of the plane. It was with his help that she wrote such exaggerations for the North Fork paper and crafted fanciful stories about Betsy and me, embellishing every move we were known or suspected to have made. In the words of the sheriff, she was after our story like a Nobel Prize.

But the sheriff overplayed it a bit. He had arranged for an airport policeman and his vehicle to be on the ramp waiting for our plane. This was designed to avoid the press, the very ones he himself had called, but, of course, he didn't tell that to the airport police. He orchestrated the whole show to make himself look like a hero returning his prize catch.

As they took me down the back stairs of the airplane, Faye Johnson came running out the door with her pen, pad, and recorder to get the exclusive interview promised by the sheriff. The airport policeman, zealous to do a good job for the sheriff, attacked Miss Johnson as he would a man, shoving her backward through the door from which she had charged. Then he called the inside airport police to have her arrested.

Meanwhile, the sheriff had gone to retrieve his personal car in the midst of bright lights from the press and the TV reporters who were scurrying to get a picture of me while the airport police and assistant sheriff put me in the back seat of the police car. All the while the embarrassed deputy was pleading with the airport police for the release of Miss Johnson, while also trying to hide the fact that they were the very ones who had invited her in the first place. The sheriff whipped around the plane in his car, picked us up and headed back to Port City, zooming in and out of traffic with flashing lights designed to simulate an emergency call. Such pretentious behavior was unnecessary but must have satisfied his ego needs.

I had lost twenty pounds and was prevented from shaving for four months. I had not even seen a mirror in six weeks, and I was still sick. Consequently, I did not want my picture splashed across the papers or on TV. Knowing that Betsy read the paper and saw the news on TV, I did not want her upset by the sight of me like this, nor did I want the rest of my family and daughters seeing me in such a disreputable, beleaguered state. I later learned that Betsy did see the news and was highly disturbed. Her lawyer asked me to write her that I really felt better than I looked.

During the ride from the airport to the jail I reflected on all the grief this man driving the car had caused my wife and me: the false rumor of the judge's payoff that prevented my innocent wife's charge from being dropped; his persistent promotion of me on *America's Most Wanted*; the contrived news coverage and treatment. Yes, he had extracted revenge, but his passion for revenge was not yet abated; there was much more to come.

Upon arrival at the jail I was closely searched, given jail clothes and shower shoes, and placed in a basement isolation cell normally reserved for overnight arrest. I was beginning to wonder if my voluntary return had not been a grave mistake.

CHAPTER 10

ASSYRIAN CAPTIVITY #2
PORT CITY JUSTICE

The morning after arriving at the Port City jail, I was informed that my overnight cell would be home for the duration of my stay. Any time I was to be removed from the cell I was to be shackled in leg irons and accompanied by two deputies, one of whom was required to be a sergeant or above. To ensure my isolation, no one could be placed in either adjoining cell, and no other inmates were allowed anywhere near me at any time. The sheriff warned his guards that their jobs would be jeopardized if they treated me with any civility whatsoever.

Thus instructed, almost all the guards treated me with contempt, refusing requests for such simple items as toilet paper or aspirin for a headache. It was over a month before I was given the broom, mop, and toilet bowl cleaner I had requested. The cell was filthy. Dried spit streaked down the walls, while the floor was covered by thick gummy crud from spilled food and other residue deposited by drunks and drug addicts over a period of many years. The stench defied description.

I was returned to Port City Jail, August 20, 1989, and Betsy was due to be tried on August 31 for aiding my escape. Because I was initially so preoccupied with her upcoming trial, I was somewhat oblivious to my environment and my own discomfort. I felt in my heart that she would be exonerated, since she was completely free of any criminal intent, and criminal intent is supposed to be more important than the actual commission of any crime—or so I thought.

Almost no one believed Betsy actually helped me escape, nor did they feel she should be prosecuted until the sheriff made it his personal crusade. Because she had not really aided my escape, I mistakenly concluded that the authorities could not convict her of doing so. She had now been in jail for three months, every day of which was a waking nightmare.

It is amazing how little most citizens know about prison life. They understand the loss of freedom but have no idea of the psychological and emotional ramifications. Fear sets in when you realize you've lost your freedom of movement, as if someone else had taken hold of your arm to guide you through doors and hallways to a destination you do not want. Every move is designed to produce submission and humiliation, beginning with the first order: "Strip off your clothes."

The second order, "Bend over and spread your buttocks," is followed by an unfriendly gloved hand grabbing your hair. Then you know that your humiliation is complete, all personal power and all dignity gone.

Next you are ordered to put on ill-fitting clothes that have been half worn out by someone else. You also receive oversized slippers that are hard to keep on your feet, thus adding to the feelings of exasperation and vulnerability. You are told you can get a comb from the canteen in a few days and you're handed a towel covered with all kinds of unidentifiable stains.

Numerous people order you to go to your left or your right, up the stairs or into the elevator. As you near the cell block, you hear loud screaming, as if someone was being hurt. Your habitat is steel and concrete, and the faces you see are full of hate.

When a barred gate is opened and you are ordered to enter, you soon find everyone staring at you. You quickly scan their faces, vainly hoping to see a friendly one. Not knowing what to do, where to sit, or where your bed is supposed to be, you feel yourself crying on the inside but determined not to let it show on the outside; instinct tells you that would be a bad move. No matter how many times you were previously incarcerated, the dehumanizing initiation process remains virtually the same.

One discovers in jail that even such things as ordinary normal body functions are difficult. Individual cells have an individual toilet, but the cell blocks have only one toilet out in the open, used in full view of all occupants. It's like having to use the toilet in the middle of your living room with a dozen strangers screaming obscenities, sounding as if they are getting ready to kill you or each other.

When meal time comes, you try to look matter-of-fact at the tray of cold, greasy food. Out of necessity you learn to eat it with your plastic spoon, no matter what it looks like or tastes like. Greasy spaghetti is always a trick, easier to handle with chop sticks than a spoon.

The tension, confusion, and noise are never absent until very late at night when tense muscles and frayed nerves finally give way to fitful sleep, plagued by nightmares. The nightmares are called "Jail house dreams" by those doing time. It seems that the night-marish existence of the waking day spills over into the chaotic sleep of the night.

Contact with the outside world was limited to three ten minute phone calls and a fifteen-minute visit each week. At that time (I believe it is better now) every aspect of prison existence was controlled by some of the most ignorant people in all society. Yes, from my previous knowledge of jail house initiation, I knew what my young, sweet, sensitive wife was going through. I laid awake at night, my heart aching for her well-being.

At that time Betsy began to study the Bible in depth, finding fresh meaning and hope in the Scriptures. Our daily letters to each other became miniature Bible studies, sharing spiritual insights and encouragement. Through suffering and sorrow, our relationship with God seemed to take on new meaning. We were discovering what really happened when God made us new creatures.

We began to see the extent of His love for us in the redemptive sacrifice of His Son on the Cross. We began to comprehend what faith, grace, and atonement are all about. In the radiant new light of scripture, we were even able to appreciate the agonizing circumstances that had brought us to such a spiritual transition.

I believe that when a person receives Christ into his life he does indeed become a new creature. *"If any man is in Christ, he is a new creature. Old things have passed away; behold, all things have become new"* (2 Corinthians 5:17).

The new creation leads to the cleaning up of old ways and personal habits which had caused previous troubles. Old problems give way to the power of God and the leading of the Holy Spirit, thus enabling the penitent to say with St. Paul, *"I can do all things through Christ who strengthens me"* (Philippians 4:13).

As recorded in the thirteenth chapter of John's gospel, Jesus taught His disciples that no servant is greater than his master. Having performed the humble act of washing the disciples' feet, He then interpreted that act to them: *"You call me 'Teacher' and 'Lord,' and rightly so, for so I am. Now if I, your Lord and Teacher, have washed your feet, you also should wash one another's feet. I have set an example, that you should do as I have done for you. I tell you the truth, no servant is greater than his master, nor is a messenger greater than the one who sent him"* (John 13:13-16, NIV).

Reading these words of Jesus in prison, I felt that He was speaking about more than an act of service. He was mandating an attitude of submission to the divine will in the face of suffering and humiliation, much like the instruction of St. Paul to his beloved Philippians: *"For unto you it is given in behalf of Christ, not only to believe on him, but also to suffer for his sake"* (Philippians 1:29). If the eternal Lord of Glory, our King, suffered for us, *"... and became obedient unto death, even the death of the cross"* (Philippians 2:8), then we should be willing to suffer for His sake.

In the midst of our turmoil, Betsy and I began to understand God's purpose in suffering. It was greatly needed in the light of events that followed. When the chief prosecutor refused to prosecute Betsy, the judge fired him and hired another lawyer as the "special prosecutor" to convict Betsy. According to the newspaper, this special prosecutor was paid seventeen thousand dollars to handle her case. To everyone's amazement, the jury returned a guilty verdict and sentenced Betsy to two years in prison.

Prior to her conviction, Betsy had been transferred back to the Port City jail where I was awaiting trial. Knowing I was so close geographically, yet unable to provide moral support by my presence, I felt intense anxiety, futility, and isolation. And so did she.

Six feet away from my cell was a steel door, with a small window in it. The door led out into a hallway used by all inmates going to and from court. I kept my eyes glued on that little five-inch-by-eight-inch window, hoping to catch a glimpse of my beloved Betsy when guards brought her back from court. Eventually, about 6:00 p.m., I saw her haggard face peer in the little window. She held up two fingers and I saw her chin begin to quiver as the guard heartlessly dragged her away.

It is hard to explain the torment that befell me. I screamed out at God. I wept. So intense was my pain, outrage, and frustration that I literally beat my head against the cement wall, hoping to gain physical relief through unconsciousness. We had thought the nightmare was ending for one of us, but instead *both* of us were now more deeply engulfed in agony than ever before.

Knowing that Betsy would want to hear that I was well and that I loved her, and knowing she would call my sister before the night was over in hopes of hearing news about me, I pled with the guards for a phone call; they ignored me. I begged with tears in my eyes, but they still ignored me.

Later that evening, when a guard stepped in front of my cell and I went to the door, he tried to cover the window by standing in front of it. I knew they would be taking Betsy back to the other jail but why did they not want me to see her? What harm could it possibly do for me to just glimpse my wife for three seconds or less?

I saw past the guard's shoulder some of my wife's hair just as a guard's hand forced her to duck when she passed the window. I could not believe anyone could be so cruel, knowing the anguish we had to be going through. Why would they go to such lengths to keep us from even getting a brief glimpse of each other? After all, we were husband and wife.

Again I persistently begged for a phone call. All that night and the next day I refused to eat until I was allowed a phone call. The guards were all indifferent except for one who snarled, "I hope you starve to death."

Then, on the third day, they intercepted a letter addressed to the newspaper, telling them of my hunger strike. It was a Sunday, and the watch commander called the sheriff at home. The guards then came and took me to the phone in leg irons. The sheriff was on the phone, speaking incoherently as if intoxicated. He told me over and over again that I would never gain anything through a hunger strike or any other such tactic I might devise.

Knowing that Betsy desperately needed some news and encouragement from me, I begged the sheriff to the point of tears to please allow me to call my sister just to find out if my wife was okay. After playing little games with me and gloating over his power and my impotence, he finally ordered the watch commander to let me use the phone and take a shower.

I called my sister and learned all about the trial, how Betsy was holding up, and what could be done. Betsy was also being harassed and having to beg for use of the telephone. She was deeply concerned about my well-being and perplexed that I had not called. I asked Sis to assure her that I was okay and I conveyed to her my deepest love, believing by faith that we would endure the anguish and separation. The example of

Christ's suffering and the promises of His Word gave us the strength and hope to persevere during those dark days.

My sister reported that even the prosecutor had expected a "Not guilty" verdict. Observers agreed that my criminal record was the primary basis of her conviction. In violation of legal propriety, the judge had allowed the special prosecutor to introduce my criminal record to prejudice the jury. With no concrete evidence of any guilt on her part, the court condoned guilt by association. Betsy's lawyer had refused to allow me to testify for Betsy because my testimony would allow introduction of my criminal record and thereby obscure her innocence. But the prosecution was allowed to do it anyhow, even in my absence.

The law does not allow a defendant's record to be divulged if the defendant chooses not to take the stand and thereby subject himself to self-incrimination. Yet the prosecutor illegally introduced my record, and Betsy's lawyer never contested the judge's acquiescence.

Following the judge's improper prosecution of Betsy's case, he refused to consider sentence reduction and added insult to injury by ordering her to serve her sentence in the Port City Jail. In the nearby county jail she had a clean bed and productive work to perform as a trusty. In Port City she had to sleep on a dirty floor among female inmates enmeshed in the drug traffic of that city.

The terrible transfer was manuevered by Betsy's lawyer, who obtained her agreement by telling her that he could get her paroled from the Port City Jail but not from the county jail. When I heard of his deception I was outraged. What little doubt I still had about Port City injustice and what little faith I still retained in its legal system was destroyed by the treatment he gave this truly innocent client whose well-being he was supposed to represent.

This laywer promised he would arrange her parole interview within two weeks but did not do so for two months. I hated the prospect of Betsy languishing in that awful Port City Jail, and I contantly worried about her sleeping on the floor among such hostile women. The sheriff, however, found satisfaction in having us under his control in his jail. The few times I saw him he exuded a gloating that clearly communicated a triumphant "'Gotcha!"

When Betsy was finally paroled on November 28, 1989, I was tremendously relieved that she finally was free to care for our infant son. Everyone in my family received her graciously, assisting her reunion with the baby in every way possible. Their warm, loving reception of her as my wife meant much to me, the greatest thing they ever did for me.

I told Betsy to be careful, obtain permission for everything she did, and keep in close contact with her parole officer. In one of her first letters after her release, she wrote, "I never thought I would someday be a paroled convict."

Her first visit to see me in jail, together with the baby, was a very emotional, bittersweet experience. I was separated from them by a bullet-proof window and had to speak through a telephone, but at least we could see each other and talk to each other. We flattened our palms against the glass together and fought back the tears. I doubt that any two people ever experienced deeper love than what we shared, yet she and I have also endured more stress, inner pain, and anguish than any other two people I know.

Our son Tucker was growing like a weed, as good a child as any parents could want. He smiled most of the time and prompted many smiles from us in return. He was healthy and extremely active from birth. Betsy had lost much weight and become entirely too thin. Although our enemies had literally taken their pound(s) of flesh, her freedom and reunion with Tucker brought the excitement and happiness needed to regain good health while becoming a model mother to her precious seven-month-old son.

Our visits were never long enough for me to gather all the information I wanted, but as time wore on, I began to notice how stressed Betsy was. Her jail experience had taken its lingering toll. Six months of constant strain, stress, fear, and depression can do strange things to anyone, especially when coupled with a sense of uselessness. After recognizing her condition, we redoubled our efforts to deal with it, both spiritually and emotionally. Betsy came to visit me on every authorized visiting day, and I called her as often as I was allowed to use the telephone, three times a week for fifteen minutes.

Both Betsy and my mother went through a very difficult transition as caregivers of the same child. During Betsy's six-month absence, Tucker had naturally turned to his grandmother as the only mother he had ever known, and she had become deeply attached to him. It wasn't easy for any of them, but Betsy and my mother were both very considerate and appreciative of each other.

My dad also had become attached to Tucker. My mother commented that he held Tucker much more than he ever held any of his own children. But because Tucker was becoming much too active for any seventy-three-year-old couple, they were both relieved and saddened when Betsy took him to a place of her own.

Betsy's stepfather, Mr. Kabler, owned a beautiful vacation home on the beach of the Atlantic Ocean, in the remote area of Beach County. He allowed her to live there rent free, a great blessing for which Betsy and I were both deeply grateful. It was the perfect place for mother and child to become reacquainted in a secure atmosphere. Hattie provided both companionship and security as the ideal, faithful watch dog. She was so protective of Tucker she wanted him in her sight at all times and became very anxious when he was not.

Meanwhile, I was becoming anxious for my day in court. My lawyers filed for access to evidence and brought me nothing but bad news. During the three months prior to my arrest in 1987, when Ox Skidmore had repeatedly visited me, he had been wearing a body recorder, seeking to involve me in self-incriminating conversations. He was constantly begging me to pull a score with him, and I was unable to get rid of him. When I refused his overtures to do a heist, he would then try to get me to talk about how I had cracked safes during previous hits.

I thought I had avoided saying anything that could be used against me, since I was then going straight, but I was horrified to hear several "spots" they had extracted from many hours of recording. Using the old vocabulary of a non-Christian ex-convict, my vile comments about my ex-wife, my brother, and others sounded offensive to any decent person. Now they were transcribed in triplicate, catalogued, and ready to be played back to a jury in a court room full of reporters, family members, friends and enemies. I felt violated and entrapped in the worst way.

All the conversations pertaining to the actual crime in question were in Skidmore's words and would have covered less than one paragraph of fifty words. The tapes would never prove that I committed the crime, but they sounded so bad that no jury could hear my verbal garbage and find me innocent. Knowing this, the prosecution pressed for playing all the tapes, and the judge granted the request.

I could have explained why I said the things I did at the time, but taking the stand and exposing my prior criminal past could have been legal suicide. I was so depressed and guilt-ridden I was almost ready to plead guilty just to avoid having those awful tapes heard by everyone in court.

My alleged guilt in this crime was based on the testimony of Ox Skidmore, the real perpetrator. To secure his testimony against me, two Federal agents arranged total immunity from prosecution, free from any punishment for this or any other crime he had previously committed. Skidmore claimed that I had persuaded him to be the insignificant "hawk" (lookout), and that he never even entered the building from which seventy-eight thousand dollars was found in his possession.

Knowing the full extent of his lies, Federal agents not only granted him immunity from prosecution, they even removed all records of his prior criminal activities from the National Crime Information Center (NCIC) except the conviction for a U.S. Postal Service safe cracking (for which he was still on parole). This was discovered by Tom Collins, a private investigator who revealed that Skidmore had eleven other convictions, most of which were violent crimes, covering a period of thirty years. The purging of his long criminal record was designed to make him appear a more credible witness against me. Port City authorities and Federal agents seemed so intent on my conviction they would even break the rules.

When I heard about these improper activities and learned what Ox Skidmore planned to say against me, I was heartsick with feelings of futility and doom. This was intensified by five months in an isolation cell and constant harassment by guards. With no daylight and no exercise, I lost weight and became weak. And with lowered resistance and poor diet, I developed a recurring flu-like malady about once each month.

In this condition, I could only imagine what a sorry sight I would be to a jury. Physically and emotionally I was winding down to the lowest ebb imaginable. Yet somehow I still had hope as I thought of Betsy and Tucker. The ever-present vision of Christ's suffering on the Cross, God-become-man, helped put it all in perspective.

It was at this time the FBI accused me of yet another crime I did not commit, this time a credit union in Indiana. After establishing my innocence of this accusation by proof of my presence elsewhere at the time, I determined that I would no longer produce proof of my presence anywhere, lest they pick a crime at a time and place that would fit their entrapment strategies. I told my lawyers that the Feds would never rest till they had convicted me of some crime, whether or not I had done it. They agreed.

"Why are they so intent on convicting me?" I asked. "What did I do to them?"

"You made them look bad, Robert. Then you insulted them with that awful letter," one lawyer answered.

While I was on escape I had written the FBI and sent copies to everyone I knew, including the governor and some other public officials. The letter voiced my outrage and objections to all they were then doing to Betsy, to my family, and to me.

"That letter was the truth," I bitterly responded, "and if I made them look bad it is because they were bad!"

I believe the Feds must have been thrilled that I was being tried in Port City; the conviction rate there was one of the highest of all the cities and counties in Virginia.

Because I had befriended Ox Skidmore when he was down and because I had never wronged him in any way, I still hoped he might tell the truth about me. And because my lawyers wanted to learn what they might expect from him, one of them went with the private investigator, Tom Collins, to talk to him in Florida. They found him very hostile, screaming threats, and leaving little doubt that he would indeed show up in court and say anything the prosecutors wanted.

When the dreaded court day finally came, I again told my lawyers I wanted to take the stand and tell the truth. The truth was bad and incriminating, but not as bad as the false charges against me. I steadfastly hoped that if I honestly told the whole truth the jury would believe me. My lawyers refused, however, insisting, "Let us do all the talking."

The first morning of court I was chained and moved to the lock-up cell behind court. One of the bailiffs was from my old neighborhood, a good man who lived his faith in the Lord. He was very kind to me that morning, taking a chair into my cell. His compassion and friendly face were a rare treat and a real blessing. From the bottom of my heart I thanked God for him and his kindness.

Court started with legal motions and jury selection. Almost all our motions, all the important ones, were denied, while all but one of the prosecution motions were granted. Through these initial rulings the judge thus revealed a personal bias and established the pattern for all subsequent trial proceedings. He ignored or discounted all the initial citations presented by my lawyers.

Trial began with prosecution's explanation to the jury as to the following: (1) What the trial was all about; (2) how guilty I was; (3) how she would prove that I was the mastermind behind the crime.

There was little doubt that most prospective jurors were familiar with my case. When questioned, most of them initially claimed ignorance but later raised their hands in response to the judge's question: "Have you heard or read about this case?" Either they did not want to appear ignorant to others, or they did not want to miss the excitement.

My case had received more publicity than any in Port City for many years. No less than fifty sensational articles appeared in the local papers, and everyone knew about my exploits. When I was returned to jail August of 1989, I received letters from people I had not seen or heard from in twenty years. One wrote that he could not pick up a newspaper without seeing an article about me.

After my appearance on three editions of television *America's Most Wanted*, after being charged with the largest heist in the history of Port City, after my escape from Port City Jail, and after the story of my wife and her alleged involvement, it was virtually impossible that these fourteen jurors who lived and worked in the same town of one hundred thousand inhabitants had never heard of me or anything about the case! Everyone in and around the case, other than the jurors themselves, agreed it was almost impossible. It was written on their faces.

The honest jurors who admitted prior knowledge were asked by the judge if it would prevent them from rendering an unbiased decision. Because no one wanted to admit prejudice, they all said "no" and were sworn in.

The fourteen unbiased jurors followed the prosecutor closely. After establishing that a break-in had been committed and that $196,000 in cash had been taken from the safe, the prosecutor displayed numerous pictures of the open safe and the damaged alarm control box. Then she really impressed them with the testimony of the two Federal agents.

The Federal agents testified that their informant, Ox Skidmore, had identified me as the culprit and that they had agreed to drop charges against him for illegal gun possession if he would testify against me. Even though the gun charge carried up to ten years, he was granted total immunity! They also admitted that they persuaded the Beach County Prosecutor to drop a house burglary charge against him in exchange for his testimony against me. When challenged by my lawyers, each agent played dumb about Skidmore's prior criminal record, hemming and hawing and finally saying, "I'm not personally aware."

The third person charged with this crime, Eddie Cantor, accused my wife of causing his arrest. I discovered later that he used this as a ploy to counteract unethical deeds he had committed against me. Actually Betsy had nothing to do with Cantor's arrest, since I did not even know her when the crime had occurred four years previously; she knew absolutely nothing about Eddie. Because Eddie was a little crazy, and because I knew from prison what he was capable of doing, I was worried by the accusation he was making against Betsy. She also was uncomfortable and apprehensive. The Feds had sufficiently prejudiced and angered Eddie against Betsy to render him a potential threat to her.

Fearful for Betsy's safety, I therefore turned to the one person I knew I could depend on to protect her from any danger—my old friend, Jimmy, known as "Wop." He had been like an uncle to me when I was a kid, and, although he had a very tough reputation, he was gentle as a lamb to all those he cared about; and he was totally loyal.

Jimmy had been a prime suspect in the murder of two court witnesses in 1973, one of whom was also scheduled to testify against me. But I don't believe he had anything to do with it. Only his reputation for being tough had made him a suspect to begin with.

I called Jimmy the week before trial and asked him to escort my wife to and from court for her protection. I should have known from all the publicity it was a bad move, but I felt it was needed. I knew Jimmy would die before he would let anything happen to Betsy, and that took a lot of worry off my mind.

When Skidmore realized Jimmy was in the court-room, he got nervous and told the prosecutor he didn't want to testify with Wop in the courtroom. A prosecution witness overheard enough of the conversation to know what was going on and told us later. Although the prose-cutor probably didn't realize how much actual harm it would cause me and probably didn't know it would get out of hand as it did, I suspect from her track record it was all premeditated.

Skidmore took the stand impressively, with all the grooming and coaching he had received, wearing a new suit the prosecutor had provided for him. After several minutes of testimony, with his eyes continually focused on the prosecutor, he suddenly said he was being dis-tracted. The effectiveness of his acting was exceeded only by that of the prosecutor, who approached the witness box and whispered loudly: "What's the trouble?"

Jurors and those in the front rows heard him say that he was being threatened with gestures. I glanced at the jury and saw all twenty-eight eyeballs focused directly on me to see what kind of threatening gestures I was making toward him. Since I was just as mystified as everyone else, I shrugged my shoulders in an effort to convey to them the message, "I didn't do anything."

My lawyers both jumped up with immediate objections and all the court broke into a stir. The judge banged his gavel and ordered the jury to leave the room. I looked at everyone in the courtroom and saw the perplexed expressions on their faces.

The Judge left the courtroom in a huff, calling one of the bailiffs behind him, and returned a few minutes later with red face and irate demeanor. The bailiff walked to the center row of the courtroom and bellowed, "Mr. Scelloto, you are hereby commanded to leave this courtroom!" He then escorted Jimmy out.

I was very upset by the episode itself, but even more upset to realize the jurors who had missed the second part would assume that I was the one accused of threatening the witness. After the jury returned, the judge began screaming threats to all my family and friends, who still had no idea what was supposed to have happened. He warned them that if they revealed so much as a smirk on their faces he would have them thrown in jail.

There were three bailiffs in the courtroom when Skidmore claimed he had been threatened, one seated beside me on my right, one seated directly behind me to prevent me from seeing my wife, and the third standing beside the jury box, looking at the witness. The judge shouted with rage that one of his bailiffs reported he saw Mr. Scelloto making threatening gestures. This seemed quite impossible, since none of them had eyes in the back of the head. During the ensuing recess several spectators reported to my lawyers they could vouch for the impossibility of any of the three bailiffs seeing Jimmy or anyone else in the courtroom audience.

My lawyer said it well: "The whole scene was the most effective use of theatrics I've ever seen played out to prejudice the jury in a courtroom."

My wife, sitting next to Jimmy, and several others seated immediately around him all swore he had never made a move of any kind. Realizing that even a bailiff was willing to twist the truth against me (unless it had been the judge himself), I wondered to myself, "Is there *any* honest person in authority in Port City?"

After the end-of-day adjournment, as I rose from my seat to be escorted back to the lock-up, I mouthed to Betsy, "I love you," and tried to smile. The next morning's newspaper article, written by the same Faye Johnson, reported that I told Betsy that I loved her and slipped her a note. This would have been impossible for Houdini, since she was over ten feet away, on the other side of the bailiff standing between us.

The sheriff went wild at this news and accosted the bailiffs, all three of whom immediately denied that any such thing had happened. They all met with Faye Johnson and she admitted it was untrue, "A mistake!" She said she *thought* she had seen me hand a note to my lawyer, and *thought* she had seen him give it to Betsy later!

Unfortunately, my wife and I were the ones who ultimately paid for this "mistake." I could no longer even mouth to her, "I love you," since a bailiff was stationed between us at all times.

My lawyers moved for a mistrial. The prosecutor argued that the jury did not hear allegations of the threatening gesture; my lawyers argued that, regardless of what they heard, jurors would naturally conclude that I was the one accused of threatening the witness. It was very obvious to everyone that jurors did hear Skidmore say he was being threatened; the court recorder heard it and recorded it in the court transcript.

The judge refused to allow any of our witnesses to testify that Skidmore's accusation was heard throughout the courtroom. He also refused to allow my lawyers to explain to the jury that it was not I who had supposedly made the alleged threatening gesture. The judge repeatedly refused to grant anything my lawyers requested.

When trial resumed, Skidmore testified that Eddie and I had broken into the Navy Credit Union while he was across the street in a motel, using a police monitor and walkie-talkie radio. Skidmore denied he knew anything about safe cracking, whereupon my lawyer reminded him of his two previous convictions for safe cracking and numerous other convictions for related crimes.

The private investigator, Tom Collins, testified that Skidmore had borrowed twenty-two thousand dollars from a bank in Florida after agreeing to testify for the Feds and had repaid the loan in less than two months — an amazing feat for a menial employee of a nursing home.

The prosecutor responded with shouts of "Immaterial!" and the judge sided with him. Because their entire case was totally based on the testimony of this lone witness, we thought his character was of great relevance.

My lawyers and I desperately wanted to subpoena Bobby, Ox's son, since he had worked for me and had performed electrical work in the credit union before it was robbed. Our lawyer wanted to reveal from Bobby's testimony that Ox Skidmore first learned of the credit union's treasure and vulnerability from his son, and then planned and executed its break-in after I had refused to participate.

As previously described, Bobby was then in the penitentiary, serving twenty years for murder. My lawyers requested the judge to issue travel orders for Bobby to appear as our witness, but he refused. By the third day of trial, I felt that I had been ganged up on and beaten half to death, both legally and emotionally.

Faye Johnson had a field day writing about the Scellotto incident, resurrecting all the old allegations of Wop's involvement in the 1972 murders and re-emphasizing my long friendship with him. Jurors were instructed not to read newspapers or watch television, but I doubt that many of them obeyed such instructions.

When I returned to jail after trial that evening, the watch commander would not allow me to go back to my cell and would not tell me why. I was exhausted and needed a bed and sleep. A deputy chained my ankle to a steel bench that was bolted to the floor immediately in front of the watch commander's station. After long protests, the watch commander ordered me unchained and transferred to the drunk tank, the filthiest place in jail, almost as bad as the one in South Carolina.

The deputies said they had orders to keep me under surveillance, using the excuse that someone thought I might try to hurt myself. Reflecting on the fact that I had never tried to hurt myself and that I had not yet been found guilty, I wondered to myself, "Do they know something I don't?"

The next morning I felt exhausted and dingy from my night in the drunk tank. Everyone acted angry, causing me to wonder to myself, "Is this because of Faye

Johnson's false report that they allowed me to slip a note to me wife? What's going on?"

After putting the chains back on me, a deputy escorted me to the holding tank behind the court room, where the first bailiff I saw was my alleged Christian friend who had been so kind to me the first day. There was joy in my heart as I anticipated kind words from a man of faith. I began telling him how glad I was to see him again, but never finished the first sentence; he coldly stared at me, turned, and walked away without a word. I concluded that peer pressure got to him: it wasn't popular to be nice to me.

My trial was a cross between a circus and a legal lynching. I have always had difficulty believing people can be truly evil and vicious, even when they are, but now I saw it incarnate; there was no one with any power on my side. I knew I was in deep trouble and might get as much as fifteen or twenty years this time. Alone in the tank, I slipped to my knees and begged God to help me.

Back in court, the prosecutor continued her harangue to the jury as to what a bad person I was. I never could understand my lawyer's refusal to let me take the stand in my own defense. Since by this time everyone knew most of the bad in my past and assumed it was probably worse than what they knew, I concluded that nothing I would say could make the situation any worse; and it might help. Unlike Ox Skidmore, I had never been convicted of safe cracking, nor of any crimes of violence anywhere at any time. My record consisted of small-time business burglaries, and my last conviction had been seventeen years earlier, in 1973. From 1973 to 1990 my only trangressions were escapes from prisons or jail.

The jury was out for deliberation only one hour before returning with a verdict of "Guilty," and a sentence of thirty years. I heard Betsy gasp and I felt faint. I was determined that I would not let her see me break. I turned and walked toward the tank with a bailiff tightly holding each arm. Because I could not risk looking at Betsy, I stared straight ahead. I was numb—completely numb, in shock and disbelief.

My lawyer requested the judge to run the two fifteen-year sentences concurrently. The request was denied, and my lawyer immediately filed an appeal. The next few weeks in my isolation cell were spent in a daze. The first phone call from Betsy was particularly painful, as both of us broke into tears. She had been crying continually since the court sentencing.

Our first visit was even worse. When I saw my son I lost control, and then Betsy also lost control. At that point, nine–month–old Tucker began to cry. Even at his young age the tender little man knew something was terribly wrong.

After composing our emotions, we decided we would not think in terms of thirty years, but rather focus on preparing our appeal during the next year and a half prior to the hearing. Numerous observers said there were many appealable irregularities in the trial and that we had a good case.

Following the trial, the newspaper quoted Betsy as having said, "They might as well have sentenced me to thirty years," and I felt she was not exaggerating; she was devastated, taking it very hard. She clung desperately to her Christian faith, trying to be strong for me. We were both clinging by our fingertips emotionally; it seemed that everything that could go wrong had gone wrong, ever since that day I was apprehended in New Mexico.

No matter how low my faith sank, I still thanked God for Tucker. Having Tucker kept Betsy busy and gave her reason to keep going. I shuddered to think how she could have endured without him; I believe both of us were capable of ending our lives without our faith and without Tucker. Life can become so bleak you don't want to face another day, when pain becomes so overwhelming you lose hope and lose heart.

The newspapers quoted one of the Federal agents as having said, "Justice has been done." I was amazed at his statement, considering I had never heard of consecutive sentencing for joint conviction of both burglary and grand larceny. I was also amazed that both co-defendants got off with *TOTAL IMMUNITY—NOT EVEN PROBATION!!* To obtain what he called "justice," this man and the other authorities had violated judicial procedures, violated my constitutional rights, and treated both of us like animals. That quote was hard to take!

My feelings toward Ox Skidmore were even more intense. When I recalled how he had originally come into my life with his hand held out for help and his mouth full of false words, how I had given him money and hired him, and how he had betrayed my kindness, I really wanted to hurt him. I didn't want to kill him; I just wanted to hurt him so badly he would wake up every morning for the rest of his life wishing he had never known me.

It was a long time before I could conquer my hate toward this depraved man. I tried all the forgiveness meditations I knew, but nothing seemed to overcome my hatred. It was not until I fully comprehended how much God had forgiven me by His slow, agonizing death on the cross that I could comprehend and apply His forgiveness toward those who had violated me.

At that time I simply tried to avoid thinking about Skidmore, knowing that eventually he would get himself into such serious trouble he could not snitch or lie his way out of it. I finally found peace by surrendering my desire for revenge to the One Who said, *"Never take revenge... 'Vengeance is mine; I will repay, saith the Lord'* (Romans 12:19)." I was very depressed over Betsy, feeling remorse that I had brought her into this hell with me, yet not knowing what to do about it. I feared how she would react if I suggested that she begin a new life through divorce. We were still very deeply in love and had grown accustomed to finding strength in each other's commitment and counsel. Our soul-bonding had been conditioned by a hunger for this deep love never before experienced, and solidified by all we had endured together. I was torn between wanting to belong to her forever, yet wanting what would be best for her during my prolonged years in prison. And beyond our personal relationship, there was no way I could give up my son.

I speculated about another escape, but swiftly realized that Betsy could not endure another binge on the lam; that would be too much to ask of her, and too much to expect from her. I said to myself, "I guess the system has beaten us after all. No matter which way I look, there seems to be no help in any direction." Thus tempered by reality, I decided to play it by ear and do the best I could, taking one day at a time.

I began this new era by deeper Bible study and prayer. Every time I felt like dying, I prayed. Following the trial, I began to discover anew just how wonderful my wife really was. Mustering faith and hope, she worked diligently to be a faithful mother to our son and a good wife to me. Although she would definitely be tested for a long time to come, Betsy had rebounded magnificently. She now faced this difficult next phase of life with a calm confidence in a triumphant God. Thus we entered our three-and-a-half-year purgatory of prison endurance and marital separation.

CHAPTER 11

TRIBULATION AND TRIUMPH

POWHATAN AND BEYOND

Not knowing what the future might hold, Betsy and I tried to identify those things that would give us hope. We even looked forward to my return to prison, since all three of us could have contact visits for several hours there instead of the mere twenty minutes allowed in Port City Jail. In prison we could talk at length and occasionally hug.

As I rode the hundred miles in the back of the sheriff's van, locked in chains, leg irons, and handcuffs, my thoughts once again turned to the possibility of escape. I believed I could do it again but did not have the zest of days gone by. To escape now would be to abandon my wife and son, or drag them from pillar to post in perpetual fear and danger; such a life would be unfair to Betsy and Tucker. Deputies in the front seat carried my papers stamped with large red letters: *"EXTREME ESCAPE RISK!"*

"Do I really have a chance in the court of appeals?" I wondered. "What would be my earliest chance of parole?" All possibilities floated through my mind, followed by unproductive speculation. I soon realized that to survive I had to stop such speculation and control my thoughts in a positive way, moment by moment, day by day. The vision I often had of release into Betsy's arms was like the climax of a movie, and it was gradually fading.

Back in Powhatan, each gate that slammed behind me diminished my hope for the future. The vinegar spray, strip searches, worn prison clothes, curt orders, rules, and regulations all accentuated the stark reality of my gloomy situation.

"Receiving Unit," located at Powhatan, has the mission of finding out who and what the criminal is, and what to do with him. This process, called "Classification," includes testing, interviewing, and medical examination. Each inmate is assigned a number and becomes a de-personalized, compliant member of the herd.

The procedure used in determining an inmate's parole eligibility focuses on the number of his previous felony convictions. Because of my previous escapes, the last of which was nineteen years earlier, I was classified a fourth-term felon, meaning I had to serve twelve years before being eligible for parole. A first-time offender with a life sentence was given the same time: twelve years.

There were many lifers, one of whom had committed terrible crimes and been sentenced to life plus 180 years, who would be considered for parole the exact same time as I. Classification personnel also select the specific prison for each inmate based on the nature of his crime, his past record of convictions and prison behavior, and his date of parole eligibility.

I called Betsy and told her when she could visit me at the Receiving Unit. She said that her parole officer could not grant permission until Powhatan authorities requested it in writing.

After many weeks passed with no request to her parole officer, I saw the assistant warden, known as "Dr. Gentry," walking past me in the cellblock. I politely explained the situation and asked if anyone could speed up approval of her visitation. I told him how anxious we were to be together again with our child, whereupon he curtly replied, "You will never have a visit from her."

"Why not?" I asked in shock.

"Husbands and wives who commit crimes together should not be allowed to see each other," he replied.

After I explained that she and I had never committed any crime together, he replied, "She was convicted of aiding your escapes; that's enough."

I angrily queried, "Is that the way you rehabilitate people, by tearing their families apart?" I was so blind with rage I had to forcefully control myself. I walked away from him quickly, believing I was dealing with a bitter, irrational, sadistic man.

I was beside myself with anger and fear. The thought of never again seeing Betsy left me with feelings of numbness and unreality. I wondered, "What other bad things can they do to us?"

I called my sister and asked her to report this to the newspapers, the lawyers, and anyone else who might help. I felt that if I didn't hear some encouraging news on the matter within a week I had nothing to live for, no reason to face such misery any longer. With this spirit of anger, bitterness, and self-pity set so deeply within my heart, God seemed to become more distant. I still prayed and still read the Bible, but the words I read and the words I spoke seemed unrelated, empty, and without enduring value.

The newspaper reporter contacted by my sister called the prison, asking if it was true that my wife had been forbidden permission to visit me. Evidently the fear of adverse publicity moved the Warden to instruct the assistant warden to authorize her visitation.

On our first visit we were able to hug each other for the first time since I left our New Mexico cabin on that awful day of April 26, 1989. I marveled at our son, as he was becoming very alert and seemed to recognize us as mother and father. He was just then taking his first steps, and I followed him around the visiting room as he explored everything in sight.

Our visits were a bittersweet mixture of joy and sorrow. The worst part was saying good-bye, as each of us groped for parting words of encouragement, abhorring the finality of the last hug. Although Betsy's visits provided joy and motivation to keep me going, they also caused anxiety and emotional pain. She drove a worn-out old car six hours each way, usually with no one other than the baby. The strain of these trips was terribly taxing on her—physically, financially, and emotionally—but she was there every week. I realized then as never before how blessed I was to have such a wonderful wife with such magnificent commitment.

Within two months I was returned to the Port City Jail for trial on the escape charge. Meanwhile, both my knees had become painful, due to immobility during my time in isolation, wearing leg irons and unable to take a normal step.

I went to see the orthopedist, who told me I had "soft cartilage. "Since he would not authorize testing and treatment, the pain increased each day, no matter what I did. Eventually I could hardly walk, thus rendering their elaborate security measures unnecessary. There was absolutely no way I could run, even if they had given me an hour's head start with no restraints.

The escape trial was a duplicate of the burglary trial. Prosecution witnesses gave false information, the prosecutor painted a false picture, and all our motions were denied. The jury found me guilty and sentenced me to three years, plus a $1,000 fine.

My lawyer objected that the sentence was not in accordance with sentencing instructions prescribed by law. When the judge realized this was indeed the case, he ordered the jury back to redeliberate, instructing them that they could sentence me to either one year in jail plus a fine, or more than one year without a fine. The jury then returned with a sentence of four years. *My God,* I thought, *they put a measly thousand dollar price tag on an entire year of my life!*

I have known many escapees who have overpowered guards, knocked holes in walls, sawed through bars, picked locks, and assaulted both guards and civilians while escaping, yet none of them have ever received more than two years. I simply walked out of the Port City Jail because of poor security and got four years!

Soon after this heartrending disappointment Betsy was hit with personal tragedy. Returning home from a prison visit with me, she was confronted by a hysterical sister with terrible news: their mother, Ceil, had shot herself with a pistol. We all knew she had been very depressed, but no one had realized how serious it really was. Betsy blamed herself. Betsy loved her mother very much, and they had been very close. I too had become close to Ceil and could not believe she was dead. I also blamed myself for all my actions that contributed to her pain and depression.

Considering what Betsy had already been through, I feared this last straw would be too great for her emotional endurance. I was afraid for her and for our son, and I was overcome with the terrible frustration of not being able to help my family when they needed me most. The funeral was small and very sad. I, of course, could not attend.

During our next visit Betsy fell into my arms and sobbed her heart out, while my heart also ached with pain beyond description. Because she was too upset to bring Tucker, Betsy had left him with my mother. So the two of us sat through several hours, trying to soothe each other's sorrow. She was so torn up I worried about her driving back home alone. I think she cried for weeks.

Soon after the escape trial it was discovered that the foreman of the jury in Wilbur W.'s trial was also foreman of my jury. Such impropriety was at least unethical, if not illegal. When the newspapers revealed this discovery, the next day's headlines proclaimed that I would win a new trial. My lawyer filed a motion for a new trial based on the discovery of the jury foreman, and they once again brought me back to the dreaded Port City Jail for the hearing.

At the hearing, the judge denied the motion, obviously reluctant to buck the Port City prejudice against me. With my bitterness and disillusionment at its zenith, I simply shrugged it off as being Port City. It seemed to me there was no other place on earth so vicious and unjust as that city.

Back at Receiving Unit, I was finally processed for transfer. I was initially jubilant with relief until I learned that my new destination was the only place worse than Powhatan—the century-old, deteriorated, overcrowded penitentiary in Richmond, where I had been beaten, teargassed, and thrown into extended solitary confinement following the tunnel escapade of 1976, fourteen years earlier.

The federal courts had ordered the penitentiary closed because it was unfit for human habitation, but the state continued operating one building that housed six hundred inmates on permanent lockdown until a federal judge later forced it shut.

With another penitentiary inmate I occupied a small cell, nine feet long, five feet wide, and seven feet high. When lying on the top bunk, my face was less than one foot from the ceiling. We were allowed out of this tiny area just one hour per day for showers and "recreation" that consisted of using the telephone. Here again, Betsy was denied visitation until we went through the same administrative ordeal as before.

Because our situation had deteriorated, even from Powhatan, I made the mistake of telling Betsy on the telephone, "Things can't get any worse. "I regretted that statement when, three days later, I was unexpectedly handcuffed and taken to segregation. I was completely baffled, since segregation was reserved for attempted escapees, prison murderers, and extreme sociopaths who repeatedly assaulted others or dealt too heavily in drugs.

I remembered that hellish place as my purgatory of suffering after the 1976 escape attempt. There all privileges and contact with the outside world were denied in both 1976 and 1990. Betsy wrote letters of inquiry and protest to the warden and others, but all to no avail. Neither he nor any other authority figure ever gave any reason for this arbitrary segregation.

Because I was so accustomed to disappointment and injustice, I no longer voiced the objection, "Hey, this isn't fair!" I merely accepted it as the normal pattern for my life and concluded that Ricochet had been correct in his 1988 warning that Satan was out to destroy me and my loved ones.

After my family threatened to introduce a law suit against the warden, I was released after thirty-two days of segregation without cause and without charges. By this time I was emotionally exhausted and too paranoid to talk to anyone around me. Because prisons always contain informers willing to snitch to guards for personal advantage, and because many of them concoct false reports about inmates whose records were as notorious as mine, I finally concluded someone had made up a false report against me. I was suspicious of everyone, wondering if my cell mate had done it to simply get rid of me and have more personal cell space. After getting to know him, however, I realized he would never do that.

Betsy and I looked forward to her release from parole, assuming that she would then be free of harassment by prison authorities. Such assumptions were proven false when, in September of 1990, she came to visit me and was refused admission. I knew something was wrong when, by noon, I had not been called to the visitation area.

After Betsy persisted in her complaint to the warden, he finally allowed an abbreviated visit *THAT DAY!* However, he told her not to return until she brought written proof that she was off parole. That seemed crazy, since she had previously obtained written permission to visit me *while on parole!* Such constant harassment was a perplexing way of life, causing us to wonder who instigated such irrational folly.

Whether or not it was stress related, my old prostate trouble began acting up again, even worse than when we were in New Mexico. For two weeks I was unable to sit on anything, even a cushion, since it had swollen to twice its normal size. I reported to sick call, was examined, sent to the Medical College Hospital, and once again given the same operation I had in Albuquerque.

After surgery, the post-op treatment was even worse than before. Only half conscious, with a catheter emptying into a plastic bag, too weak to even put on my shoes, I was fastened in handcuffs and leg irons by cursing guards.

In terrible pain, I was surprised to learn that instead of returning me two miles back to the penitentiary, the guards were hauling me forty miles away, to the Medical Holding Unit of my old nemesis, Powhatan! During that agonizing trip I was forced to half stand in the van, with my head against a wire mesh grate in order to catch myself when the brakes were applied. Such a stance prevented the tearing out of the catheter, but was very painful. The jolting and moving around during that terrible forty-mile trip produced bleeding and serious complications that left me in worse shape than before the operation. I then realized I must learn to care for myself, and I began reading about prostate and bladder functioning. I adopted a vegetarian diet (which was very difficult in the prison setting), and began a regimen of regular exercise. All provided some relief, but left me in pain.

After two weeks in the Powhatan Medical Unit I was transferred to the Powhatan general population. At the very time I had been in surgery at the Medical College Hospital, a federal judge had issued a decree forbidding the old penitentiary from accepting any new inmates—

the first step toward its ultimate closure. I doubt that the judge intended his decree to cause additional pain by preventing the return of a recovering patient, but some prison official interpreted it as an opportunity to do so. Thus I was permanently displaced without retrieving my few personal belongings from the old penitentiary.

Again back at Powhatan, I was given a cell with an inmate six feet, three inches tall who weighed 270 pounds; they called him "Big Red. "The only difference in my new cell and the old one in Richmond was a higher ceiling, thereby allowing me the luxury of sitting up on the side of my bed.

Time dragged on as we waited for my appeal. Finally, on January 28, 1991, a year after my trial and nearly three-and-a-half years after arrest, my appeal was heard by a three-judge appellate court. My lawyers predicted an answer within thirty to sixty days, but I was too leery of the judicial system to believe them. Consumed by bitterness and depression, my Bible found its way to the bottom of my belongings, and I seldom read it any more. My prayers grew less frequent, muttered out of a sense of duty.

Recognizing my spiritual delinquency, several well-meaning Christian friends from the free world gave me advice, cliches, and hard luck stories about the suffering of others. This left me feeling even more miserable and isolated than before. I understood in a personal way the pain Job's friends inflicted on him at the very time they thought they were consoling him. I only hoped to attain his unique patience and ultimate triumph of grace.

Engulfed in isolation and self-pity, I was blinded to the fact that my troubled life was the result of my own past choices. Early in life I had chosen to rebel against my family, school, church, community, and God, all in that order. Considering all I had done, I was lucky to even be alive; no, not lucky—blessed!

Before God enabled me to open my eyes, I had always focused on the injustice of everything. I accentuated how unfair it was that had I suffered terrible prison experiences back when I was a teenager; how unfair it was that Ox Skidmore and Eddie Cantor, both with long, evil records, had been granted total freedom, while I, a non-violent criminal, was saddled with the equivalent of a life sentence. I thought how unfair it was that Betsy had endured such abuse for simply standing beside me as a loving, loyal mate. How unfair it was the sheriff and his people had treated me with such cruelty, etc., etc., etc.

While in such a state of despondency, I was ordered to the captain's office and told to call home. Remembering that the last time he sent for me I was informed that Betsy's mother was dead, I silently cried out from my heart, "Please, dear God, let my wife and son be okay!"

On the telephone I learned that my dad had suffered a stroke and was paralyzed. Listening to my younger brother describe his condition was more than I could bear. I turned to the wall to hide my face between the payphones, so that no one would see the tears streaming down my cheeks. My dad and I had had many differences, primarily due to ignorance by both of us. Despite our inability to communicate, I knew he loved me, and I loved him. He had cared for me when I was young and tried to set me on the right path in life.

Remembering how Dad always had been such a conscientious hard worker, it was painful to visualize him now as a helpless invalid. I told my brother to tell him I loved him, that I would be praying for him, and that I wanted to see him again. I was ashamed of the ill feelings I had held in my heart toward him for so long.

Two months later I was called to the captain's office once again for another dreaded telephone call. Again the silent cry of my heart, "Please, dear God, let my wife and son be okay!" This time it was my lifelong friend, Sonny. Although we last parted with bad blood between us, I knew we would eventually straighten it out as we always had. But I had waited too long, and now it was too late. My heart was heavy with remorse; I could hardly believe he was gone after all we had been through together. I was the godfather of his daughter, and it was through him I had met and married his niece—my beloved Betsy.

Like his sister, Betsy's mother, Sonny had also committed suicide. He had taken a cab to the beach at Sandy Ridge, walked out into the ocean with a pistol, and shot himself. More than once I had heard him say he wanted to be buried at sea: "I want to be food for the fishes and crabs." He always loved the ocean, where he had worked and played most of his life. He was the stuff Jimmy Buffet wrote songs about. Many times I had seen him drunk, singing those Buffet songs he knew by heart with the gusto of a Buffet man.

After I met Jesus Christ I had often prayed for Sonny, that he too would find redemptive peace. I wondered if perhaps in his last conscious moment of life Sonny might have called on God. I hoped so with all my heart, feeling deep grief and deep regret.

In April 1991 the Virginia Court of Appeals granted my appeal on four of the five contested issues. The media made this sound like my case was being overturned and I would soon be out. Actually, it only meant that I had won the right to carry the appeal one step further for another hearing. After another six months of motions and rebuttals the same court heard the case again and was scheduled to give a ruling in three to five months. After five months and no word, all the unpredictable happenings seemed insane.

In the midst of such intense frustration, heartache, and insanity, something marvelous began happening to me that provided a spiritual "second wind." It was as if God had finally completed the step-by-step agony of brokenness and was ready to begin His step-by-step remolding of the potter's clay. After Betsy and I "bottomed out," God introduced several people and four activities to reveal His grace.

First there was the veterans' group. Mike Paley, a former Marine Corps Gunnery Sergeant also incarcerated in Powhatan, organized the Vietnam Veterans of America Chapter 682. Dr. Floyd, who had met with the veterans in James River Prison prior to recall to active duty during Operation Desert Storm, had again retired from the army and become a volunteer consultant for the Powhatan veterans. He recruited another Vietnam veteran, Gray Taylor, a teacher at Thomas Dale High School in Chester. Gray became External Sponsor of the Veterans Chapter. Although I had not served in Vietnam, I was accepted into membership of this remarkable group.

Then came the Prison Fellowship Seminar sponsored by Charles (Chuck) Colson. In that seminar we studied the biblical concept of forgiveness, and the Lord laid on my heart that Ox Skidmore was not the only one I had not forgiven; I also needed to deal with my hatred for society as a whole. With help from some Christian brothers who prayed with me, I was finally able to forgive all those who had wronged me. Whether my opinions of them and their actions had been just or unjust, a tremendous load was lifted from my heart and

I was able from that point on to grow spiritually as never before.

The third group was composed of like-minded inmates who met in the prison kitchen for informal Bible study. With no elected human leader, these caring, committed men sought the Holy Spirit as their Leader. Because other Bible study groups included inmates seeking to misuse previous groups for their personal advantage, I joined this group with great caution until I found them motivated by a spirit of genuine Christ-like grace. The majority of participants were black, and their contagious good will helped dispel my lingering racial prejudices. We related Bible knowledge to our daily life struggles and gained a sense of freedom in sharing our struggles as Christian brothers.

The fourth activity was a conventional Bible study in the prison chapel, conducted by two wonderful, mature Christians, Mr. and Mrs. John Wickstead, known affectionately as "Alex" and John. Leaders in St. Giles Presbyterian church, Richmond, their weekly Bible teaching imparted keen insights and spiritual maturity. Their outstanding service also extended beyond prison visits and Bible study, as they periodically took former inmates with no place to go into their home for weeks of Christian hospitality during the crucial period of transition back into society.

While participating in these four activities, I still experienced spiritual and emotional resistance. Because I had always rejected anything psychological as "baloney," and "bunk"—stuff to be avoided—I wanted to skip the "Rap Sessions" Gray Taylor started with VVA Chapter 682. But since I had been elected secretary, Alan Mackey, our president, and Mike Paley gently pushed me to fulfill my duties, saying, "Come on, we need you there."

Each week I reluctantly but dutifully attended the sessions, vowing beforehand to remain silent. As Gray skillfully challenged me and other shirkers, however, I would find myself denouncing societal injustice with bitterness. After this happened several times, Alan Mackey confronted me with my hostility: "Is this the same Robert Witt who's been telling me about the love of God?"

Deeply embarrassed by such truthful assessment of my contradictory statements, I sought Mike Paley and Gray Taylor to apologize for my tirade. Gray, whose muscular six-foot-four-inch frame had been a dominant force when he played college football, reached his arm around me, gave me hug, and said, "It's okay, R. C. You're doing just what you need to do. God loves you, and so do we."

I was overwhelmed by this response. As a child, I had worked hard to earn my father's acceptance by being good, but somehow never could. As a teenage hustler and an adult criminal, I worked hard to be the smartest and most effective crook, expecting thereby to gain respect and acceptance from other offenders. Instead, they usually just used me. NOW, while spewing out bitter resentment among my Christian brother-veterans, they overlooked my foul mood and accepted me as a person of worth in spite of it.

Back in my cell, I reflected on this momentous, insightful event. Accepted by the veterans' microcosm of society, I now finally felt truly accepted and affirmed. I realized that what had happened on the human level was a marvelous reflection of divine forgiveness and acceptance; the response of Gray Taylor, Mike Paley, Alan Mackey, and other group members came from hearts touched by the grace of God.

Back in my cell, reflecting on this moment of truth, I slipped to my knees and prayed, "O Lord, I don't understand why You have allowed so many terrible things to happen to me and my loved ones. You know how much I hate being cooped up in this prison, and You know that I cannot go on this way. If you want me to spend the rest of my life in prison, I am willing to do it. I just ask You to give me Jesus' peace, so that I can be faithful, the instrument of Your redeeming love."

It was then, on the deepest level of encounter, that the invitation and promise of Scripture was experienced: *"With thanksgiving, let your requests be made known to God. And the peace of God, which passes all understanding, will keep your hearts and minds in Christ Jesus"* (Phillipians 4:6b-7). Since that time, God has nurtured me with an abiding peace that permeates the trials and frustrations that would have previously set me off in rebellion.

I also received encouragement and gained insight from individual counseling with Dr. Floyd and from the psychological assessment he provided veterans at Powhatan. During one session he asked, "R. C., what can I do to help you?"

Initially I responded, "Nothing. My two year old son will graduate from high school before I can ever walk the streets and be a real father to him."

After reflection, however, I added, "On second thought, you could call my wife and try to give her some words of encouragement." This he did, beginning a supportive ministry to her with periodic telephone conversations every two or three weeks. Although he and Betsy did not meet for another two years, those telephone conversations undergirded her with a sense of well-being and hope that blessed her. And it meant much to me as well.

During this period I experienced new spiritual insight. It became obvious to me that God had broken and humbled me, leading me to cry out for mercy. Romans 3:11 makes it clear that without God's initiative no one has the motivation or wisdom to know Him. Yet, in times of catastrophe, even unbelievers spontaneously cry out "O God!" as an involuntary reflex.

While reflecting on all this, I was amazed to read in Deuteronomy that God had led the children of Israel for forty years of wilderness wandering in order to humble them. (Deuteronomy 8:2) I had thought that two hundred years of slavery would have humbled them sufficiently, but their Egyptian bondage only produced rebellious murmuring. Wilderness privation and wandering was necessary.

It is by the grace of God in suffering that He prepares our hearts for repentence and invites us to accept His forgiveness. He then pays the penalty for our sins, remolds and reshapes our lives. Not everyone goes through the crucible to such a degree as I, to be reshaped and remolded, but even to this day God gets my attention quickest when things are bleak. As stated in II Corinthians 12:9, His "... *power is made perfect in weakness.*" Paul himself was given "a thorn in the flesh" to keep him humble. (II Corinthians 12:7-10.)

But the Lord didn't just break me and leave me to put myself back together. Almost daily it seemed He sent someone into my life to address certain issues from my past. Dr. Floyd played a big part in this with personal counseling and psychological assessments. When I first met him I wondered what was in it for him. Surely he had better things to do than drive forty miles each way to visit a bunch of convicts in prison. But as I got to know him I could see that he was compelled by the love of Christ.

During this time I also developed a tremendous hunger for God's Word and for Christian fellowship. Even though prison life was still overwhelming and hope for freedom flickered dimly, the second wind of inner peace and spiritual joy permeated my soul and transformed my journey from a steep uphill climb to a level walk.

One day in October 1992, while standing in line waiting for the loud speakers to call our cell block for dinner, I felt an impulse to call home. I was standing beside telephones that were almost always in use, but were all suddenly and amazingly free. I called Betsy, hoping she was there, while mentally scolding myself for running up her phone bill.

After answering she said, "Guess what, honey?"

"What?" I replied, realizing how happy it made me feel just to hear her sweet voice.

"I have beautiful feet," she said with pride.

Oh, this is it, I thought, fearing that Betsy had finally gone over the edge of sanity. Why in the world would she be telling me she has beautiful feet?

"Uh, yeah," I muttered, searching for words. "Sure Babe, I've always known you have beautiful feet."

"No, you don't understand. The Bible says in Isaiah 52:7, 'How beautiful are the feet of those who bring good news,' and I have some really good news: THE COURT OF APPEALS OVERTURNED YOUR CONVICTION!" she proclaimed with great excitement.

It took a second for the news to sink in. I suddenly felt light-headed. I dropped the telephone and fell to my knees on the cement floor, exclaiming, "Thank You, Jesus!"

In my peripheral vision I noticed several men step back, thinking I had gone crazy. Perhaps it was the sound of that name, "Jesus. "It is, after all, the Name that has caused more controversy in the last two thousand years than any other name under heaven.

"R.C., R.C.," I could hear Betsy's voice over the dangling telephone.

I grabbed the phone and got to my feet. "What does this all mean?" I asked.

Betsy began to relate how she had heard the news. The husband of her friend had been riding to work and heard it on his car radio. He stopped and called his wife Karen, and Karen called Betsy. She called my sister and my lawyer, neither of whom had heard the news. Karen then called her husband Bill at work, to get the name of the radio station. Betsy called the station and they replayed the news to her over the phone. It was days later before the lawyer heard anything from the court of appeals.

By this time I had served over three years, which would easily satisfy the four-year escape sentence. I wondered how long it would take them to release me.

Several days later a guard came to my cell and said I would be leaving in the morning. He did not know if I was to be picked up by authorities. The next morning Port City authorities were there to get me.

Port City had decided to retry me. The case had been overturned because the judge had erred in not declaring a mistrial when the witness on the stand (Ox Skidmore) claimed he was being threatened in front of the jury, thus preventing me from receiving a fair trial. Unknown to the appeals court, the newspaper had in fact reported that members of the jury admitted that episode had weighed in their decision. Now Port City planned to simply try me all over again.

The thought of going back to Port City Jail was very depressing to me. Then my lawyer informed me he was withdrawing from the case because he wanted more money. Betsy and I were stone broke and owned no assets other than the old car she was driving.

The lawyer further told me on the phone that he saw no way for an acquittal, that I should take a ten-year deal if they offered it to me, as he expected they would. When I asked him to at least try to get a bond set, he chuckled and asked me if I really thought they would really grant a bond I could ever raise. Actually, considering that my first bond was a quarter of a million dollars prior to my escape, I didn't really think they would give a reasonable bond. But I was grasping at straws.

The mention of ten years came as a shock to me. Did he know something? What about Skidmore and Cantor who went free? What about all I'd been through? My agony should count for something.

Then the words "Trust Me" came to my mind. I did not know how it was going to all work out, but I believed God's hand was in it. Just days earlier I had read the Scripture in Jeremiah 29:11: "'For I know the plans I have for you,' declares the Lord, `plans to prosper you and not to harm you, plans to give you hope and a future.'"

One week after being returned to Port City I was taken before the judge to have a lawyer appointed. When they brought me into the courtroom I saw Betsy and my sister, Brooke, sitting close to the front.

The judge shuffled some papers and asked me, "Do you have any way to retain a lawyer, Mr. Witt?"

"Your Honor, I have no money to hire a lawyer, nor does my family have any money to hire a lawyer."

"Do you have any assets, Mr. Witt?"

"None, Your Honor," I responded. "I have lost everything I ever owned and I do not have one penny."

"Well then, the court will appoint you a lawyer."

A public defender stood up and said, "Judge, I'll take this case."

"Are you sure you want this case, Mr. Underwood? Are you familiar with this case?"

"Yes, Your Honor," the public defender replied. "And, Your Honor, there is a matter of a bond here. My client, Mr. Witt, deserves a bond like anyone else, and I would respectfully request the court to set one."

I was thinking I was really going to like this guy; he had heart, that was for sure.

"Okay," the Judge responded, "I'll set a fifty–thousand–dollar bond."

I could hardly believe what I was hearing! I asked the bailiff standing next to me, "Did he say fifty thousand dollars?"

The prosecutor quickly jumped to his feet. "Your Honor, I object!"

"I've set the bond!" the judge curtly replied. "And that's it! And furthermore, I am removing myself from the case. I was involved in the last trial."

I turned and looked at my wife and sister, as they both were holding their hands over their mouths with a look of shock. They whispered to me as I was being led away, "We'll get you out."

It took them two days of persistence, but my sister finally obtained a property bond by putting up her home as collateral. I was released ten minutes to five on a Wednesday afternoon, December 9, 1992. All of us were in tears as we departed the clerk of court's office. We quickly made our way to the car, my sister giggling as she always does when nervous, and Betsy and I holding each other tightly. It was as if we wanted to hurry out of there before they changed their minds.

We went to the babysitter's house in Beach County, the home of Karen and Bill, the ones who had first heard the news and told Betsy. As I walked through the door, my three–year–old son, who was sitting on the floor playing with his friend, Chris, looked up at me and asked, "Daddy, what are you doing here?" He had never seen me outside the prison visiting room, and this scene was strange to him. Then he ran into my arms and gave me a big hug. Suddenly he stopped, looked me in the eye, and asked, "Daddy, do I really get to keep you now?"

With tears in my eyes and a lump in my throat, I said to him, "Yes, my son, you get to keep me now," yet wondering if, in fact, he really would.

DELIVERANCE AND FREEDOM, 1993

While waiting for court to begin, October 8, 1993, six years after my arrest for the credit union theft, reflections of my teenage struggles that had continued over thirty years of crime and spiritual awakening suddenly gave way to the awareness of legal reality. If the judge approved the proposed one-year deal, I could serve six or eight months, then return to my family and begin life again with a fresh start. I reasoned that this was a million times better than the thirty-four-year sentence I was serving before the court of appeals overturned my conviction.

During the ten months following my release I awakened every morning with joyful amazement, realizing that I was actually free. By contrast, while in Powhatan Prison, I had begun each new day praying for hope and encouragement to merely endure. Now, anticipating a one-year sentence, I could plan for lasting freedom in just six or eight months. Yet, even while anticipating the relief this deal would bring Betsy and me, anxiety still lingered. When the anxiety seemed to reach its peak, I could feel in my heart and hear in my mind those two penetrating words: "Trust Me!"

When court came to order, everything happened much quicker than I could have imagined. The bailiff read the charges just as he had four years earlier. The judge then asked me how I would plead. With my heart racing wildly, I managed to get the words out, "Guilty, Your Honor." This was the first semblance of admission of guilt I had ever spoken!

The prosecutor stood and recommended a one-year jail sentence. The judge accepted the recommendation and sentenced me to one year. He and the prosecutor then departed almost as quickly as they had entered; everyone was relieved it was over. As the bailiff led me away, I glanced back at my wife, remembering how I was unable to do so four years previously. I saw her tears combine with a smile of encouragement.

My lawyer, knowing that something was up, told my family and friends to wait a few minutes before they left. As I was being processed at the jail, a deputy approached me and said, "Mr. Witt, with good time you're required to do 180 days for a one-year jail sentence. According to our computers you have done 181 days in our jail while previously waiting to go to court. You will therefore be released as soon as we finish this paper work."

I never even saw the inside of a cell that day. In less than forty-five minutes I was totally free, with no strings attached! As I heard in my mind the echo of "Trust Me," tears welled up in my eyes. In total contrast to years before, everyone I encountered, from bailiffs to the last deputy, was extremely nice to me. I once again marvelled at the truth of Proverbs 16:7: " When a man's ways are pleasing to the Lord, He makes even his enemies to be at peace with him" (NAS).

It was hard to believe that just a year earlier I was serving a thirty-four-year sentence, with little hope for the total freedom now granted. When I returned to the courtroom, it was through the front entrance, without any bailiff at my side. As the door swung open, Betsy, my sister, and my friends appeared bewildered. The fantasy came to pass after all! Betsy ran into my arms; victory and freedom were ours! Another miracle!

A new journey then began, one whose paths wound through discipleship training, marital adjustments, the birth of another child, and many struggles and trials. At each crossroad I continue to see the truth of Philippians 1:6: "Being confident of this, that He who has begun a good work in you will carry it on to completion until the day of Christ Jesus" (NIV). Just as it was never in me to look for the Lord on my own initiative, it has never been in me to grow spiritually on my own. Christ began the good work when He broke me, humbled me, convicted me of my sins, and reconciled me to God through the redeeming power of His crucifixion. The Lord's work did not stop with reconciliation, however. Just as we are saved by grace as described in Ephesians 2:8-9, so we also grow in grace. It is only in retrospect that we understand the wonder of it all. God uses every circumstance in our lives to produce in us the new creation described in 2 Corinthians 5:17.

The journey is incredible. The Enemy has managed to completely misrepresent and obscure the true meaning of the Christian life. Here in America, Christianity is portrayed as a bland, socially acceptable religion whose adherents are narrow-minded, dull, and spineless. The real truth is just the opposite. A truly biblical lifestyle is very fulfilling, but not socially or politically in vogue. Described in the Old Testament as "a peculiar people," we are the few and not the majority. We are instructed to "enter by the narrow gate; for the gate is wide, and the way is broad that leads to destruction, and many are those who enter by it. But the gate is small, and the way is narrow that leads to life, and few are those who find it" (Matthew 7:13). Our belief in the awesome power of God focuses on the heart of Christianity—incarnation, crucifixion and resurrection—and cannot be fathomed in a narrow mind nor experienced by a timid spirit.

The born-again Christian is constantly changing with growth and new light coming into his or her life daily. Putting on the mind of Christ, as described in Scripture, and living with Him and for Him is the most exciting journey that can ever be traveled in this life. And the journey takes more courage than anyone alone can ever muster.

After three years of freedom Betsy, our seven-year-old son, Tucker, our two-year-old daughter, Hannalore, and I live in a small, beautiful home in the country. We relish spending time together, and we have a deeper appreciation for one another than the average family who has never experienced the pain of separation. It amazes me what the Lord has done in our lives.

In addition to my work as a master electrician and Betsy's multiple work as housewife, mother, and college student, we are very active in jail and prison ministry. I have spoken at schools, churches, banquets, jails, and Powhatan Prison, from which I once escaped. On different days she and I lead Bible study classes in the local jail. By telephone and by correspondence we encourage many inmates across the state of Virginia to persevere in faith.

We have heard from men and women in prisons who have been humbled, broken, and then cried out to God for help, claiming the promise of His Word that He will hear the cry of the prisoner (Psalm 79:11 and 102:19,20). Now many of those very prisoners are praying for the authorities who harass them. They also pray that society as a whole will be humbled and seek God. Many Christians believe that when true spiritual awakening finally comes to modern America it will begin in our prisons.

There are two extreme attitudes in America today toward crime and punishment. On one extreme, well-meaning, idealistic, altruistic people excuse the criminal too quickly. They minimize lawless trangressions of the individual by claiming that society as a whole is respon-sible for all the wrongs of everyone: "The criminal is only reacting to the victimization society handed him in such a bad environment." Such naivete is ridiculous.

The opposite extreme, increasingly popular in America today, advocates a vindictive and merciless hatred for inmates: "They're all rotten and always will be. Lock 'em up, throw away the key, and sock it to 'em while you've got 'em." Such diatribe has secured the election of many politicians and become the prevailing philosophy of many professionals in corrections. It is as irrational as beating a caged dog so that he will not be mean.

Between these two unproductive extremes there is a sane middle ground advocated by Christians and other enlightened citizens. This middle position is even-handed, first nailing the transgressor to his responsibility with the admonition, "You have done wrong, you must pay for it, and you need to change both your attitude and your behavior."

Such somber words of reality are then followed by words of hope and encouragement for the penitent: "But the future can be different. And we will help you learn to make it better if you are willing."

One of the saddest things to witness is the plight of a penitent offender whose penitence is ignored or discounted. I have witnessed numerous instances where rejection of the penitent's confession caused him to feel demeaned and more resentful than before.

Those politicians and citizens who take great pride in being "hard on crime" often miss the point. The rising crime rate is not due to authorities being too soft on crime, but rather to our pervasive societal immorality; the absence of ultimate moral and spiritual values creates a vacuum that invites criminal behavior. Moral and spiritual standards expressed in both law and grace produce better results than vindictive law enforcement and penal harassment.

Betsy and I plan to invest the remainder of our lives ministering to the incarcerated, eventually full-time. Upon graduation from college next year, she hopes to become a professional counselor to female inmates. I hope to begin theological studies, earn a degree, and be ordained a prison chaplain. As this writing goes to press, we do not know how my studies will be financed, but we truly believe that "With God all things are possible"(Matthew 19:26).

CRIMINAL BIOGRAPHY OF ROBERT C. WITT

April, 1964 - ARRESTED at age 15 for one count of grand larceny of an automobile in North Fork, Virginia, and one count of grand larceny of an automobile in Mount Airy, North Carolina. After two months of incarceration, sentenced to one year probation.

JANUARY 3, 1966 - ENLISTED in the U.S. Marine Corps and sent to Parris Island, South Carolina, for twelve weeks of boot camp.

JULY 1966 - ARRESTED for breaking and entering a restaurant in North Fork, while on three day liberty from duty station in Memphis, Tennessee. After forty days in jail, charge reduced to petty larceny and sentenced to one year suspended and turned over to the Marine Corps. USMC pressed charges for absent without leave (AWOL). Confined in Camp Allen Brig in Norfolk.

July, 1966 - ESCAPED from Camp Allen Brig and re-captured the same day. Two weeks later transferred to Brig at Camp Lejeune, North Carolina, and remained incarcerated for two months.

October 31, 1966 - DISCHARGED from the Marine Corps with Undesirable Discharge.

April, 1967 - ARRESTED in North Fork for possession of stolen goods and released on bond.

June 10, 1967 - MARRIED Sandra at Beaufort, North Carolina, while out on bond.

June 22, 1967 - SENTENCED to three months for possession of stolen goods.

June 26, 1967 - SENTENCED in Noth Fork to the one year in prison for violation of probation in previous conviction of July 1966. Total sentence: fifteen months. First long incarceration begun in Powhatan Prison (formerly "State Farm").

January 10, 1968 - BIRTH of daughter, Robin Michelle.

March 26, 1968 - RELEASED from Powhatan Prison to freedom.

April. 1968 - ARRESTED in North Fork for alleged 1966 breaking and entering. Charge proven false and released.

May, 1968 - ARRESTED for driving without a license.

May, 1968 - ARRESTED for alleged disorderly conduct.

May, 1968 - ARRESTED for forgery, issuing and passing of worthless checks. Released on bond.

July, 1968 - SOUGHT on Federal warrant issued for unlawful flight to avoid prosecution.

November 24, 1968 - CAPTURED in Virginia, by Federal agents.

November 26, 1968 - CHARGED with thirteen counts of commercial burglary in Virginia and one count of commercial burglary in Nansemond County.

January 2, 1969 - BIRTH OF second daughter, Joyce Elizabeth.

February, 1969 - CONVICTED of check cashing fraud in North Fork and sentenced to two years there.

February, 1969 - REMANDED to Suffolk Jail for the Nansemond county burglary trial. CONVICTED and SENTENCED to five years in Nansemond County.

March, 1969 - CONVICTED and sentenced to ten years in prison for thirteen burglaries in Virginia.

August, 1970 - ESCAPED from road camp in Halifax, Virginia, and captured the same night.

September, 1970 - SENTENCED to one year for escape.

September, 1970 - DIVORCED by wife, Sandy, while incarcerated.

October, 1970 - ESCAPED from road camp in Tazewell, Virginia.

November, 1970 - SOUGHT on Federal warrant issued for unlawful flight to avoid confinement.

March 27, 1971 - CAPTURED by Federal agents in Richmond, Virginia. Unlawful flight charge dropped.

May, 1971 - SENTENCED to one additional year for Tazewell escape.

June, 1971 - TRANSFERRED to maximum security at Powhatan Prison.

November 26, 1971 - ESCAPED from Powhatan Prison.

September, 1972 - CAPTURED in North Fork and handed over to Port City for prosecution on nine counts of burglary.

January, 1973 - SENTENCED to eight additional years in Port City court and returned to State Penitentiary in Richmond.

March, 1973 - TRANSFERRED to Powhatan Prison.

August, 1973 - CHARGED and SENTENCED to one additional year for possession of a knife.

September, 1973 - TRANSFERRED back to Penitentiary in Richmond.

October, 1973 - SENTENCED in Richmond to additional one year as a habitual offender.

June, 1976 - CHARGED with attempted escape from Penitentiary.

November 26, 1976 - GRANTED PAROLE and posted bond on attempted escape charge.

January, 1977 - FOUND NOT GUILTY by a jury in Richmond Court for charge of attempted escape.

February, 1977 - ARRESTED in Virginia Beach for attempted burglary and released on bond.

March, 1977 - SENTENCED to three years for attempted burglary and transferred to Powhatan Prison.

March, 1978 - TRANSFERRED to Deerfield Correctional Center.

January, 1981, - PAROLED.

September, 1984 - MARRIED second wife ("Martha").

January, 1986 - COMPLETED PAROLE after five years of crime-free living.

May, 1986 - SEPARATED from second wife.

July, 1986 - BEGAN DATING Betsy.

September 17, 1987 - ARRESTED for the February, 1986, burglary of the Port City Naval Credit Union.

September 21, 1987 - ESCAPED from Port City Jail.

September 8, 1988 - MARRIED Betsy Kabler in Pensacola, Florida, while in fugitive status.

October 7, 1988 - REDEEMED By JESUS CHRIST as Savior and Lord while still a fugitive. (Praise God! Thank God!)

April 17, 1989 - BIRTH of son, Tucker, born in Tijeras, New Mexico, while still a fugitive.

April 26, 1989 - CAPTURED in Albuquerque, New Mexico.

May, 1989 - BETSY SURRENDERED to Federal authorities in North Fork and incarcerated.

August, 1989 - EXTRADITED to South Carolina, to stand trial for alleged armed robbery of a credit union there.

September, 1989 - EXONERATED in South Carolina after charges were proven false and dropped.

September, 1989 - EXTRADITED to Port City, Virginia.

September, 1989 - BETSY CONVICTED of aiding escape and SENTENCED to two years.

November 28, 1989 - BETSY RELEASED on parole.

January, 1990 - CONVICTED and SENTENCED to 30 years for the credit union burglary.

February, 1990 - TRANSPORTED to Receiving Unit, Powhatan Prison, and incarcerated in State Penitentiary after "Classification".

March, 1990 - RETURNED to Port City for trial regarding 1987 escape. CONVICTED and SENTENCED to four additional years.

September 29, 1992 - RELEASED after thirty year conviction of 1990 was overturned by the Virginia Court of Appeals and REMANDED to Port City Jail.

December 15, 1992 - RELEASED on bond, pending retrial in Port City Court.

October 8, 1993 - PLED GUILTY in closed court presided over by a judge without jury trial. SEN-TENCED to reduced term of only one year. Because time served in Port City Jail while awaiting trial in 1990 satisfied requirement for a one year prison term, RELEASED a free man!!! By the grace of God!!!

To order additional copies of

An Inside Job

please send $11.95
plus $3.95 shipping and handling to:

Robert C. Witt
P.O. Box 746
Chester, VA 23834

*Quantity Discounts are Available